A BIRDWATCHIN
COSTA BLANCA

MALCOLM PALMER

598.0723446765

I.S.B.N. 09522019 41

First published 1993
Revised edition 1994

Arlequin Press, 26 Broomfield Road, Chelmsford, Essex CM1 1SW
© Malcolm Palmer/Arliquin Press

All rights reserved. No part of this book may be reproduced, stored in a retrieval system or transmitted in any form or by any means, electronic, mechanical, photocopying or otherwise, without the permission of the publisher

A catalogue record for this book is available

CONTENTS

The Province of Alicante 4

Neighbouring Provinces 6

Travel to and around the Province 8

A selection of Birding Sites in the Province 12

Systematic List 22

Conservation in Alicante 47

Species Checklist and Spanish Names 48

References 54

INTRODUCTION

The idea of writing a guide to the birds of this small and under-watched part of Spain grew, quite gradually, from a series of discoveries. The first was that the Province of Alicante is, in effect, a microcosm of virtually all the habitat-types to be found in Eastern Spain, and the realisation that it occupies a prime position, on a busy migration route. The second was that there is no guide, in English, which helps the would-be birding visitor to find birds in the area. The third was the amount of interest shown by people I have met, and who have had the use of our little house at Santa Pola. Lastly has come the dawning of knowledge that we have here a very special area. The discovery of Spain's fourth Wilson's Phalarope was a start, soon followed by a wider understanding of the occurence-pattern of species like Caspian Tern and some of the rarer gulls. Later came the finding that the winters hereabouts could be very exciting indeed, with some huge gatherings of waterfowl, and more than a scattering of rarities. In recent years, the spread into the Province of Cattle Egret and now White-headed Duck have merely served to underline this 'special' status.

I hope this little book will serve to challenge people to further study, and perhaps even do a little to cause the authorities to awaken to the need for coherent and integrated conservation measures. We read and see much about 'Green Tourism'. Here is a golden opportunity for a Government to encourage development of Reserves and other initiatives, and to help save the remnants of a once-vast wetland area before it is too late.

There are plenty of good field-guides on the market, and, for this reason, I have made no attempt to deal with identification, nor has there been any intention to instruct the reader in matters of breeding-biology, behaviour or any other aspect of birdlife, all of which are best left to weightier publications, but I trust a small gap will be filled by this necessarily incomplete work.

MALCOLM PALMER, 1992

(Note: The scientific names of all birds mentioned in the text are given in the systematic list).

Foreword to the Second Edition

After the best part of a year's continuous birding in the area, it soon became clear that there was a need for a greatly-enlarged second edition of this book.

Accordingly, I have incorporated much information gleaned from local reports (credited in the references) and from both personal observations and discussions with other enthusiasts. This has resulted in what is a much more complete work. There are, however, no grounds for complacency, and I anticipate confidently that the current list of species will be extended to over 300 in the next, say, five years.

Work remains to be done on the populations of even the commonest species, and, due to the paucity of local birders, any help that can be elicited from visitors will be gratefully accepted.

Malcolm Palmer, Santa Pola.

THE PROVINCE OF ALICANTE

Alicante is a small but immensely varied Province, situated on the southeast coast of Spain, and known to millions of holidaymakers as the Costa Blanca.

Nowhere is the Province much more than 60 kilometres wide, and its total length is only around 130 kilometres, but its deeply indented coastline probably has a length exceeding 200 kilometres in all.

For such a small area, the diversity of habitat is quite remarkable. In general, the main areas may be summarised thus:–

a) The High Sierras
b) The Wetlands
c) The Coast
d) The Agricultural Plains
e) The Lowland Pinewoods

Each of these areas in turn contain considerable diversity, which may well account for pockets of distribution of species found in the Province.

a) The High Sierras

Roughly the northern half of Alicante Province is mountainous, largely consisting of young limestone mountains which make for dramatic serried peaks and crags, often with abrupt cliff-faces, ideal for cliff-nesting birds such as Chough and Crag Martin. The valleys are often fertile — result, no doubt, of the heavier rainfall attracted by the mountains — and are usually fairly intensively farmed. Just in one or two places, however, there are extensive patches of woodland, which act as 'oases' for breeding birds and migrants alike. Many of the Sierras are cloaked in pinewoods, and these support bird communities much like those found throughout Spain. Others take the form of bare, rocky hillsides, and, whilst they are only sparsely populated, may hold some of the more interesting species of the region.

Sierras jut out southwards to the west of Crevillente, but these are generally less dramatic in character than those further north, and tend to be less well supplied with potential nest-sites, though one small area is potentially highly interesting. Many of the Sierras present difficulties in terms of access, and the wildlife communities are, in consequence, imperfectly known.

b) The Wetlands

This area represents comfortably the most important portion of the Province as far as wildlife is concerned, when viewed from an overall perspective. There is one important wetland in the north of the Province, namely the extensive reedbed north of Pego, and there are the derelict salt-pans at Calpe, but the vast preponderance of wetland in Alicante is in the southern half of the region.

The main wetland areas will be described under 'Sites' headings, but it is worth mentioning here that the two main areas have entirely different characters, El Hondo being a remnant of a once-vast area of marshland, and the Santa Pola marshes formed as a result of salt-extraction, though doubtless also a remnant of original saltmarsh. The two areas are sufficiently close together to have a regular interchange of birdlife.

Only some low hills and a few kilometres of largely agricultural land separate these wetlands from the two salt-lakes of La Mata and Torrevieja, and again some interchange occurs, particularly at passage times.

The ditches and dykes of the often marginal agricultural area provide some wetland 'mini-systems', offering feeding and nesting facilities, particularly to passerines.

A 'less important' stretch of water is the Embalse de la Pedrera, an extensive reservoir in the hills between San Miguel de Salinas and Orihuela, which is deep and steep-sided, and seldom holds major bird-populations, though often attracts migrants.

c) The Coast

The coast itself is only of interest in a few places, and human activity, usually in the form of unchecked touristic and residential development, has rendered much of it sterile from a wildlife viewpoint.

In the north there are a few stretches, notably between Denia and Aduanas, and between Costa Nova and Moraira, where access is limited, and it is possible that a few cliff-nesting species can survive, but further research is required. Benidorm Island, just off the famous holiday resort, is an important site for breeding birds and occasionally passage migrants.

The entire coastline from Calpe south as far as Santa Pola is then heavily developed, and such reaches of sandy beach as there are have long been dedicated to tourism. Southwards from Santa Pola, resorts are a little wider-spaced, and, at least in winter, a few shorebirds are allowed to rest here and there. Dense development is again to be found around Torrevieja. Offshore, the island of Tabarca, some four kilometres off Santa Pola, has relatively undisturbed coasts outside the main tourist season, and there are a few rocky stacks too.

The main ornithological interests on the coasts, however, are twofold. Firstly there is the sea-passage, and several headlands can be excellent for observing the comings and goings of a surprisingly rich variety of seabirds, especially when strong winds blow in off the sea. The abundance of marine life also means that good numbers of seabirds feed close inshore in winter.

Secondly, the coastal areas sport some very good habitat for migrants in spring and autumn. The dunes of the southern coasts, around Guardamar, are heavily cloaked in woodland — usually mixed palm and pine — and such areas are well worth checking for migrants at appropriate times. Some rocky headlands, such as the Cabo de Santa Pola, are also sufficiently remote from residential districts to hold bird-communities of their own, but here again development is an ever-present threat.

d) The Agricultural Plains

The triangle with the city of Elche at its northern point, the mouth of the Rio Segura to the southeast, and the town of Orihuela to the southwest is almost all reclaimed marshland, now given over very largely to agricultural production, with cereals, potatoes, peppers, artichokes, asparagus, cotton, onions and many other crops being grown, often with the assistance of extensive irrigation systems. This ensures that there are many dykes and canals intersecting the area, often giving rise to patches of reed and papyrus. These make for little 'oases', and are often quite rich in birdlife.

The open fields are most productive, from an ornithological standpoint, in the winter months, when many are left for grazing by some substantial herds of goats and sheep.

e) The Lowland Pinewoods

To the south of the agricultural areas, much of the remainder of the Province, as far as the southern border, consists of low, rolling hills, often intersected by river-valleys, which cut deep little ravines in the clay soil.

A large proportion of this country has now been planted with citrus groves, and is internationally important for production of lemons and oranges. The citrus groves themselves hold good populations of some species, notably Serin, but extensive spraying of pesticides must be a limiting factor.

The low hills which remain cloaked in pine trees are important for their population of the elusive Red-necked Nightjar, and the banks in this area can often hold colonies of Bee-Eaters. Some of the region is quite difficult of access, and there may yet be discoveries to be made here.

In between the habitats described, there are vast areas of more-or-less marginal land, with some stony wastes in the south, often relatively birdless, and extensive upland plains in the west, much of which area is dedicated to vineyards.

Near Villena in the northwest of the Province, is a relic of formerly extensive 'steppe' country, where one or two typical species may still be found.

In some cases, human activity has provided unexpected niches for wildlife, and coastal towns make for artificial 'cliffs' of interest to Black Wheatears and Blue Rock Thrushes, whilst a few buildings make homes for Pallid Swift as well as more common species.

The overall impression a newcomer will get is one of a wide diversity of habitat in a restricted geographical area, and the value of this may be seen when viewed in the context of Alicante's position just a short distance from the North African coast, and quite definitely on a major migration route.

NEIGHBOURING PROVINCES

It is not the intention of this book to cover in detail the birdlife of neighbouring Provinces, but some appreciation of what may be found there may well offer the possibility of a day-trip (or longer) and may also point to the possibilities of occurence of some species occuring in nearby regions.

The territory to the west of Alicante Province is largely typical of mainland Spain, with big agricultural tracts interspersed with areas of broken ground, often in the shape of forested hills. The mountains to the northeast of Cuenca constitute a vast area of wild country, and should repay a visit.

Just south of the Madrid road some 100 kilometres northwest of Albacete is a low-lying marshy area containing the Laguna de Manjavacas, which has turned up good waders in recent years.

Some three hours' journey to the west, the Sierra de Segura sports several species of eagles and vultures, as well as other montane species, and is just about as close as one can be to see the exquisite Azure-winged Magpie *Cyanopica cyana*, which breed on the western slopes of that range.

Most of the 'day-trip potential', however, lies immediately to the south of the Province, in Murcia Province.

At the northern extremity of the Mar Menor, just over the provincial border, lies an extensive area of working and disused salt-pans, and these can be viewed from the road around the northern edge of the inland sea. They contain all the birds one would expect of such an area, and are well worth a visit.

A very good spot is south of Alhama de Murcia, near the banks of the Rio Guadalentin. Take the MU 602 towards Cartagena. Near the crossroads after 7 kilometres, take any of a variety of tracks towards a man-made reservoir surrounded by an earth 'bund'. The salicornia contains Calandra, Short-toed and Lesser Short-toed Larks, Stone Curlew and Black-bellied Sandgrouse, and Rollers breed in the area. A nearby bridge, on the MU 603 near Casas Nuevas usually holds a colony of Red-rumped Swallows, and the area has held Little Bustard in at least one recent winter.

Some way to the west of this is the village of Aledo. To the left of the MU 503, just after the junction with the road into the Sierra de Espuña, an area to the left of the road has been a breeding site for Dupont's Lark in recent years.

The Sierra de Espuña itself is an excellent spot. Breeding birds include Golden Eagle, Peregrine, Alpine Swift, Rock Bunting etc., and the wild Mouflon, a unique race of Red Squirrel and many butterflies make this an ideal venue for a day-trip from Alicante, served as it is by a fast road, by-passing Murcia.

Further to the south, Trumpeter Finch have been found in the Sierras around Cartagena, and the coast around Mazarrón is worth a look.

If planning a longer trip, the 'Spaghetti Western' country of Almería Province is very 'atmospheric', consisting of arid desert, holding Thekla Lark, Stone Curlew, Trumpeter Finch (with luck!) and not a lot else. The occasional patch of vegetation is, of course, interesting in this sort of place, and Rollers and Bee-Eaters can be found almost anywhere.

The Cabo de Gata is a fine sea-watching spot, with Rock Sparrows and the possibility of a Bonelli's Eagle in the area. The nearby salt-pans are excellent, with big Audouin's Gull roosts, and the wide coastal wilderness just east of Almería airport has flocks of Black-bellied Sandgrouse. The delights of Granada, the Sierra Nevada and the other wonders of Andalucia are not such a long way away now, as the road southwestwards has been upgraded, and a morning's drive will see you well on the way to that unique part of Spain.

The above is not meant to be in any way a comprehensive guide, but will hopefully whet the appetite for further exploration. This entire corner of Spain is probably under-studied from a wildlife point of view. Many naturalists from Northern Europe have made a bee-line for the superb region of southwestern Andalucia, but as the Coto Doñana becomes increasingly threatened, and the danger of 'doing it to death' ever more real, it may be no bad thing if more birders turn their attention to new areas. There is plenty in and around Alicante to challenge the enquiring visitor!

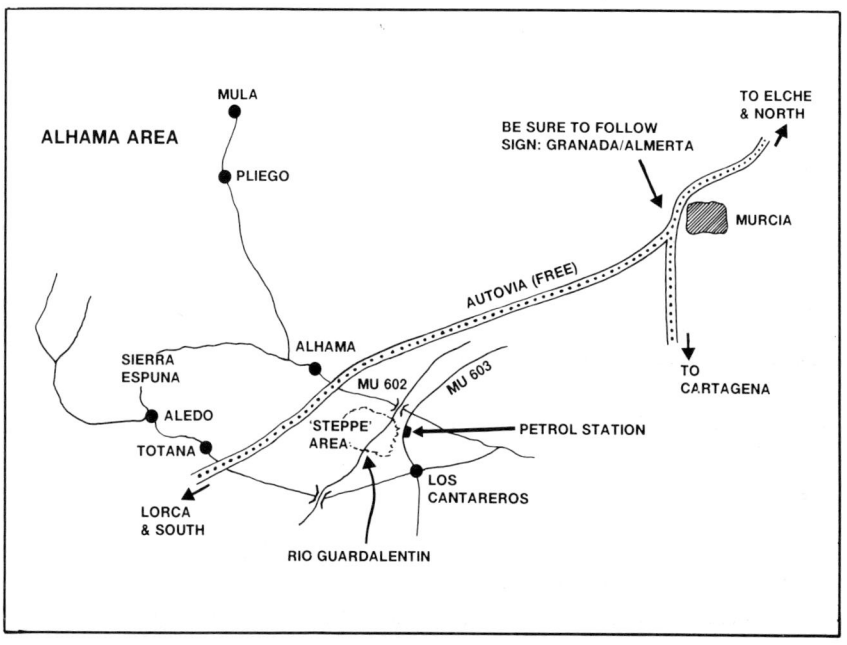

TRAVEL TO AND AROUND THE PROVINCE

One of the great beauties of Alicante as a birding destination is its accessibility. The immense number of Northern Europeans who maintain holiday homes in the Province gives rise to a vast number of cheap, year-round charter flights to Alicante, which take around two or two-and-a-half hours from the United Kingdom airports. These can be booked through travel agents, or simply by telephone to one of the many 'bucket-shops' or ticket agencies.

The only blot on this system is the relatively high price one has to pay to travel at school holiday time, when fares may rise by as much as 50%. An alternative is to drive down from the north, but this is a relatively long job, and not practicable unless you have at least a fortnight's holiday. Then it can be an enjoyable experience, weith some excellent birding *en route*, especially in the Pyrenees. The roads are almost all good, but do beware of motorway tolls, which can add a good deal to the cost of your trip.

Another option is to take the ferry from Plymouth to Santander, then drive across Spain. This should not be viewed as a cheap alternative, but may well be a very pleasant diversion.

Having arrived at Alicante airport, much the best thing to do is to have a hire-care waiting for you. This can be done very simply, by dint of a telephone call from the UK. Many charter-flight operators will also book you a car when you reserve your flight.

Unless your car-hire is prepaid, you will need to have sufficient pesetas to pay for it on arrival. Even if you have paid in advance, you will probably have to pay in local currency for a tankful of petrol. (You take it back empty). Incidentally, beware of paying by credit-card for your car, as some companies levy a surcharge for this service.

The cheapest cars are usually quite adequate for two or three people, but afford only scant security, and it may be better to hire a car with a boot, especially as you may wish to leave optical equipment in a secure place on some occasions.

In this connection, it may be worth mentioning the epidemic of theft which has swept Spain in recent years. Foreign or hired cars are seen as a particular target, and it goes without saying that precautions ought to be taken, especially with optical gear, cameras and radios. Good insurance may well be the only real safeguard — and do read the small print!

Roads and signposting in the Province are generally good, but towns are often labyrinthine, and seem reluctant to release the unwary traveller, at least on the right road out. The standard maps are the Michelin 1:400,000 No. 445, which covers all of southeastern Spain, and the Firestone *'Mapa turistico'* 1:200,000 T-28, which just covers the Costa Blanca. This is adequate for most purposes, but the Spanish equivalent of the Ordnance Survey publishes a 1:50,000 series of the whole area, which are extremely good for detailed study. They have not, however, been updated since 1974, and are also rather expensive, unless you wish to concentrate on one small area.

Of the other ways of getting about, a bicycle may well be the best option, especially in the lowland areas, although the main roads would be a less-than-peaceful experience, and summer temperatures are not conducive to physical effort. Many mountainous areas, and some remote reedbeds, can only be reached on foot, and the mud in some of the latter locations can be especially cloying after rain, so Wellington boots may be worthy of consideration, except, perhaps, in summer.

Weather

The climate of this part of Spain has often been described as near-perfect, from a holidaymaker's viewpoint, and it is certainly a place to go if you enjoy sunshine.

Although, as elsewhere in Europe, some variety is inevitable, the rainfall between June and mid-September is negligible, and tends to take the form of the occasional violent storm. Outside these times, October and November are very variable and December and January can be quite wet, but usually allow plenty of time between the rain for birding. There tends to be a mainly dry spell in February and March, with some more unsettled conditions through April and May.

Winds are seldom very strong, at least by Northern European standards, but stormy conditions can and do bring some almighty gusts at times.

Temperatures can be extremely high in summer, when it is barely possible to go out birding between, say, 11 a.m. and 5 p.m., and travel by car is akin to purgatory. In spring and autumn, conditions are normally ideal for birding all day, whilst winter temperatures tend to resemble a pleasant spring day in Britain. It can, however, be very cold at night, and in the early hours of the morning.

Accommodation

There are plenty of reasonable hotels throughout the Province, and a sufficiency of campsites. Booking is unlikely to be necessary, except in high summer. A package-deal holiday to Benidorm may be one way that the newcomer may be initiated into what Alicante has to offer, but it will be necessary to escape the clutches of the resort before any serious birding can be done.

A better option may well be to seek accommodation, on a self-catering basis, in one of the thousands-upon-thousands of holiday homes close to the best birding areas. Many people will know of a friend or relative with one of these, but failing that, contact the author of this guide, at:

> Calle Javea, 43,
> Gran Playa,
> 03130 Santa Pola
> Tel: (from UK) 010-34 6-541 13 10
> From April 1995 00 34 6 541 13 10

Alternatively, details may be had from:

> Calandra Holidays, on (UK) 0223 628547
> From April 1995 01233 628547)

Food

There is no need to be concerned about food! Restaurants abound throughout the Province, and prices are seldom as high as you may think from a glance at the outside. The food is generally very good, especially if you like seafood, although there is plenty of variety in the main centres.

Delicious snacks can be found in bars, in the form of tapas, at any hour, and the less adventurous will find hamburgers and sandwiches readily available.

Supermarkets are found everywhere, and stock a wide selection of foodstuffs, and prices are broadly similar to those throughout Europe, except that the excellent local wines, and all fruit and vegetables, are very cheap.

Water, incidentally, is perfectly safe out of the tap, though many now prefer the taste of the bottled variety.

Local People and Customs

The people of Alicante consider themselves Valencian first, and Spanish a poor second. This means that they speak Valenciano, which is a dialect of the Catalan tongue spoken right up as far as the French border, and having its capital in Barcelona.

This gives rise to the usual defacing of Spanish roadsigns, especially in the mountainous areas, and you will see many notices in two languages — not unlike Wales! The two are not, however, a million miles apart, and everybody is able to speak good Castillian (Spanish).

Away from Benidorm, Torrevieja, and a few other resorts, however, it is often hard to find anyone who speaks English, and the visitor who learns a few words of Spanish will find himself at some advantage, as local people will see this as a sign of respect.

There are areas where access is much restricted, and this is often due to hunting interests. Trespass is to be actively discouraged, and may well invite the attentions of a green-uniformed guard, who has instructions to see you off the premises. The golden rule, as elsewhere, is 'If in doubt, ask', and most places can, in any case, be seen well enough without resort to commando tactics.

Hunting is important to a lot of Spanish people, and it is worth considering whether disturbance to wildlife is worse in that country than in Britain, for example. At least the visitor to Spain is spared the spectacle of organised fox- and deer-hunts!

There is a new interest in wildlife in evidence, and Spanish television has produced first-class wildlife films in recent years. You actually see Spanish birders in the field now, and it is not unusual for conservation issues to be local 'hot potatoes', debated in the local press.

It is possible, then, that the birding visitor will come into contact with local enthusiasts, and a knowledge of the scientific names of all species likely to be met with may prove invaluable, unless you are taking the trouble to learn the Spanish ones!

Otherwise, the only contact visitors tend to have with local people is often concerning food. Mealtimes are traditionally late in Spain. Breakfast is a rudimentary affair, often consisting of churros, or doughnuts, small sweet buns and coffee and/or cognac. This may well be taken standing-up in a bar. Lunch is traditionally a long, lingering feast, never before 1 p.m. and often starting as late as 3 p.m., going on until perhaps 5.

An early evening drink may 'put you on' until dinner, which is never before 9 p.m. and may be started as late as 11.

This 'laid-back' and rather leisurely attitude to mealtimes is in tune with the climate, and a midnight feast under the stars, with a good day's birding behind you, can be an unforgettable experience.

Almost all restaurants put tables outside in the summer, but it may well be too hot to take lunch in the open, and many locals retreat into the air-conditioned interior during the heat of the day.

Should you chance to visit the Province in late December, the custom at Christmas is far removed from that of Britain. Restaurants are closed on Christmas Eve, when people have family-gatherings, but open on Christmas Day, although all the shops are closed for the day only.

New Year's Eve is the big night out, when all the restaurants have amazing (and amazingly expensive) banquets, and nobody goes to bed.

This apart, there is a plethora of fiestas, which may occur without warning to the uninitiated, and ensure that there is no supply of fresh bread, and that the banks are closed. It is as well to check locally for this eventuality at the start of a holiday.

Seaside Holidays

It is likely that many birders will be attracted to the Costa Blanca by the dual possibilities of birding and taking the family for a seaside holiday. Although wives tend to see through this ploy, there are fine beaches for the kids, plenty of attractions such as water-parks, safari parks, horse-riding establishments, excellent sports facilities, windsurfing schools and so on.

Benidorm is known universally as the capital of the package-deal holiday, and there are good resort facilities at such places as Torrevieja and Calpe, to name only two.

Santa Pola is like a Spanish version of Bridlington circa 1953 in the height of summer, with dodgems and candy-floss, ice-cream parlours and boat-trips, and not a lager-lout in sight.

Bathing is generally safe almost anywhere on the coast, and scuba-diving opportunities exist in many places. The cities of Alicante and Elche, and the many regular local markets, afford good bargain-hunting, especially for shoes, which are made around Elche, as well as lace and the local speciality turron, a type of nougat.

In conclusion, the whole area is excellent for a family holiday, and at prices which even those with a young family should be able to aspire to.

A SELECTION OF BIRDING SITES IN THE PROVINCE

In order to show the location of the sites mentioned, the map of the Province is divided in two. One showing sites north of Alicante, the other showing sites to the South. The location maps are intended for guidance only and show main roads. It is recommended that a suitable road map is used on conjunction with this guide when touring the sites. [NB. The Michelin Map No. 445 — Levante, Valencia–Murcia is one such map and the Michelin map reference is shown in brackets alongside each site title.]

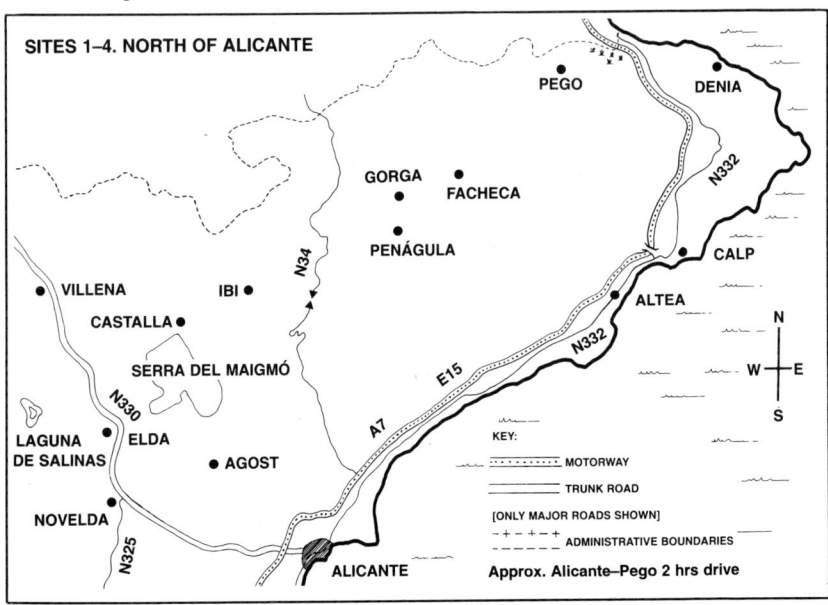

1. **PEGO** (map ref. P29)

The most northerly extent of the Province is marked by some really extensive reedbeds. Visible from the coastal motorway, halfway from Gandia to Denia. They may be

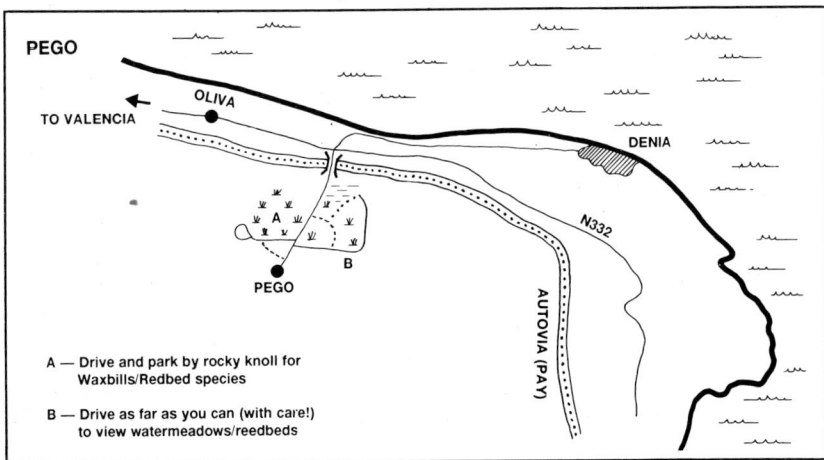

approached most easily from the town of Pego to the south, or from the coastal road, the N-332, from the north. Taking the latter route, it is necessary to turn southward on the VV-1066, just over the provincial border, in Valencia Province, then cross over the motorway. It is then possible to take a left turn along an unmade road leading to a pile of stones, from where some very good watermeadows can be viewed. These, however, can be seen to better advantage from the opposite side, requiring a drive right around the reedmarsh, on reasonable tracks. The reeds themselves hold a good variety of birds.

On the right-hand (west) side of the VV-1066, there are more reedbeds, and low hills bordering them, where the feral flock of Waxbills seem to be holding their own. All around Pego are some fine mountains, and the valleys are often very good for woodland species.

2. CALPE (map ref. Q30)

The disused salt-pans right beside the main road to the large rock (the Peñon de Ifach) are almost always home to perhaps the most easily-accessible Audouin's Gulls anywhere, and all you need to do is to stop by the roadside and look across to the old causeways of the salt-workings. A few waders and terns may also be about.

The rock itself may be worth a walk, and Crag Martin and Peregrine would be worth looking out for, as well as any migrants in the fields on the way up.

Not far away, at Altea, the coastal highway (N332) passes over a bridge to the north of the town. Underneath passes a watercourse, with many areas of reedbed, which may teem with birds at migration-times, and in winter, when Bluethroat are usually to be found here.

3. GORGA/PENAGUILA (map ref. P28)

This area is generally not untypical of the northern Sierras of the Province, but has the added advantages of a stand of mature deciduous trees, and an accessible cliff-face.

Just outside the village of Penaguila, the road swings sharply around a corner, by an obvious rocky ravine. A short walk will confirm that Chough and Crag Martin breed, but no raptors, other than Kestrel seem to be in this area, though who knows . . . ?

On the way north to Gorga, a well-wooded river-valley can be approached on two different roads. The lesser of the two is the more interesting, and a big stand of mature poplars and other trees make a change from the pine-cloaked hillsides. Here Spotted Flycatchers and just possibly Robin breed, and a longer stop may well reveal other species. The road northeastwards, through Facheca, is wild and interesting, with good views of some high crags, where Rock Sparrow are well established.

4. SIERRA DE MAIGMÓ (map ref. Q27)

Maigmó is just a matter of 20 kilometres from Alicante, on the road to Ibi. If, however, you approach from the south, the road from Agost (not well sign-posted) is interesting, with a Crag Martin colony near the top of the hill, and Golden Eagle have been seen in this area. Just after the parting of the ways, where the Ibi and Castalla roads divide, take a left turn into the Nature Reserve. The road is precipitous, and not for the faint-hearted, but, in its lower stretches it is quite gentle, and there are plenty of places to stop in the pinewoods, for Crossbill, Crested Tit, Rock Bunting, Coal Tit and other specialities. The top of the road gives stunning views, and some good crags are around the head of the valley.

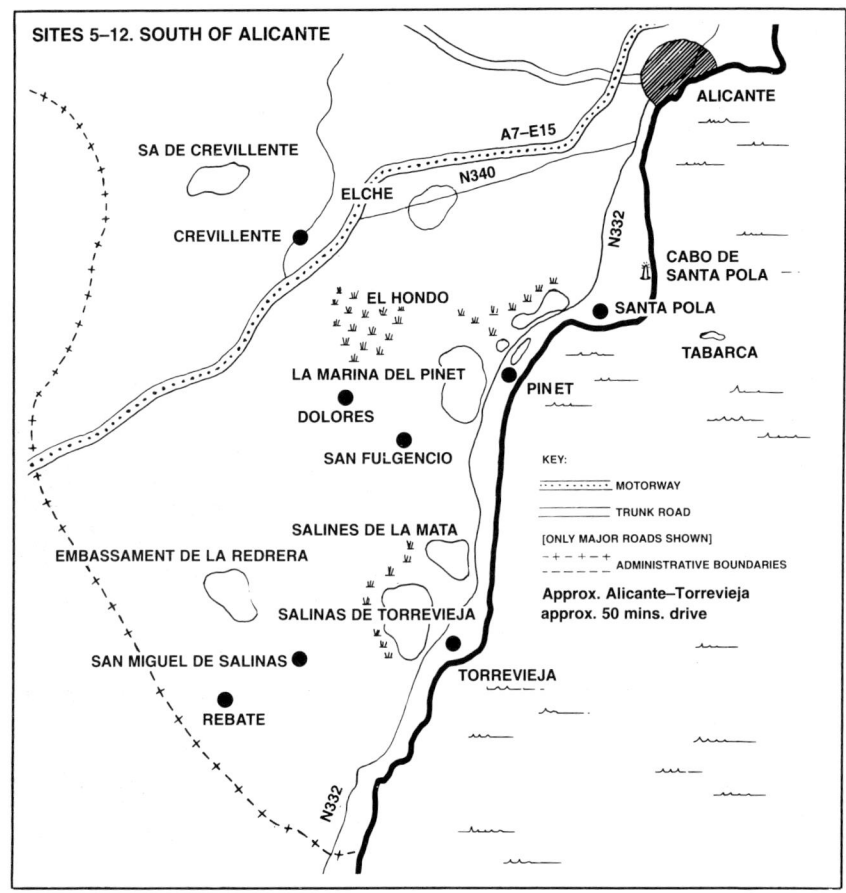

5. CABO DE SANTA POLA (map ref. R28)

A small and diminishing area, this, and probably no better than a lot of similar spots, but the combination of coastal location and wild country lend an attractiveness. Simply turn east off the main coastal highway 3 kilometres north of Santa Pola. About 1 kilometre along on the left, walk a little way in amongst the pines, and you will come to a deep ravine. This area is good for shrikes, and Rufous Bush Robin breeds fairly commonly. The scrub is quite good for warblers all the way to the Cabo lighthouse, where migrants may be found. The cliffs have Black Wheatear and Blue Rock Thrush.

6. TABARCA (map ref. R28)

This is the small island you can see from the previous site, Cabo De Santa Pola, some 4 kilometres offshore. It can be reached by pleasure boat, from Alicante, Torrevieja, or, most conveniently, from Santa Pola. The trip takes half an hour, and is not expensive. The biggest drawback is that your visit is restricted to the middle portion of the day, and that it may not be possible to get across at all between late October and mid-March, with the possible exception of weekends. It would, however, be possible to camp on the island,

The extensive salinas of Santa Pola are the major feature of the area. This area provides suitable feeding for thousands of birds and not least for Flamingos.

The marshes at Pego some two hours drive north of Alicante are worth a visit for its great variety of wetland species whilst its propensity to produce rarities to the area on a regular basis makes it doubly attractive. During the winter months Bluethroats haunt the reed beds.

The mouth of the river Segura lies just north of the picturesque town of Guardamar. Though recently embanked with stone along both sides it is still a haven for birds. An elevated road either side of the river allows easy viewing over the water, while the boardering fields and citrus groves offer plenty of opportunities to observe various passerines, Shrikes and Bee-eaters etc,.

Cabo de Santa Pola, haunt of Rufous Bush Robin.

which would be helpful at passage times. Accommodation could also be sought at the numerous restaurants etc.

The village occupies the whole western end of the island, which is about two kilometres long, and is of ornithological interest only because Pallid Swift and Rock Dove breed in the massive church.

The wild eastern end has a veritable forest of Prickly Pear, and some scrub in the fenced lighthouse garden. These areas are worth checking at migration times, and are often full of warblers, flycatchers and wheatears. Short-toed Lark breed in good numbers. The rocky stacks off the eastern tip can be viewed from the little cemetery near the point, and Audouin's Gull probably breed there. The rocky shores often hold waders, and the sea-watching can also be good.

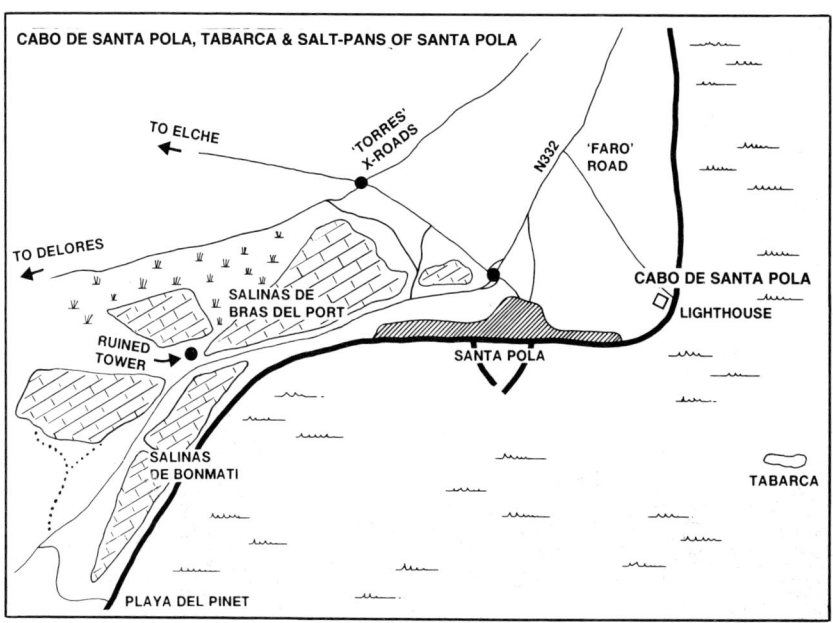

7. THE SALT-PANS OF SANTA POLA (map ref. R28)

This is an area of perhaps 25 square kilometres, centred on three working salt-extraction operations, stretching southwards along the coast from Santa Pola to almost La Marina, and inland to the wilder reedmarsh, marked on the map as the Albufera de Elche.

As with many other such habitats in the Mediterranean Basin, the working areas are of variable use to birds, often only supporting flocks of roosting gulls, which line up along the narrow causeways between the lagoons. These in themselves, however, may be of interest, and the big gathering of Audouin's Gulls are relatively easy to find. Take the rough road which skirts the northern edge of the salinas, almost opposite the road to Playa Lissa, and joins the Elche road. About 200 metres along, there is a left turn, up a little hump. Stand at the top of this, and look over the salt-pans to the west, and the Audouin's are about 100 metres away. The old, disused salt pans in this area are also good, especially for waders.

Southwards along the coast road, you will come to a ruined tower in the middle of more disused salinas. In this area look out for Marbled Duck, which are, however, remarkably shy at some seasons. Other birds in this location are too numerous to mention individually, but the road is a constant problem, except on Sunday mornings, when there are no birds, at least in winter, due to hunters!

The entrance to the Bonmati saltworks is another spot where a stop is worthwhile. On the opposite (west) side of the road, it is possible to get off the road, and walk a little way towards the lagoons, and this is where the numbers of Flamingo, Avocet and other waders can be quite enormous. Perhaps the best thing to do is to park near the advertising hoardings on the right a little further towards La Marina, and then walk down the track to the edge of the lagoon. Here some excellent watching can be done without the disturbance of the traffic — but a telescope is essential!

The 'back' of the salinas can be approached quite easily, by taking the Elche road from La Marina. Go over the bridge and around a sharp bend, then park just beyond a building on the left, and walk along a track to the right, bordering a big area of *Salicornia*. This track leads right into the back of the wildest areas, and good views of some remote lagoons can be gained. In winter, this area holds lots of Marsh Harriers and Crag Martins, and the field round about may also have big Lark flocks.

8. EL PINET (map ref. R28)

This is a little resort immediately to the south of the Salinas de Santa Pola, and could almost have been considered under that heading, but it does have some more specialised aspects, so has been taken to be a separate site.

Travelling south from Santa Pola, take a left turn just after the filling station before La Marina, and follow an unmade road to the point where it crosses a scrap of reedmarsh. Here is a good place to look out for rails and crakes. Bear round to the left, and a good view of the extreme southern salt-pans unfolds. Here there is a good chance of Slender-billed, Audouin's and Little Gulls, as well as terns.

The beach at El Pinet is good for sea-watching, as well as bathing, and the dunes just behind are often teeming with migrants. Butterflies are also to be found here.

9. EL HONDO (map ref. R27)

To any Spanish-reading visitor to El Hondo, the book by Navarro Medina is to be vigorously recommended (see Bibliography), as here only an outline of this unique place can be attempted.

El Hondo is an area of reedmarsh, shallow lagoons and dykes, taking up a tract of land between Dolores to the south, and the tentacles of the city of Elche to the north. The marshes have, in common with those all over Europe, diminished greatly in the last 50 years or so, and the inroads of agricultural and other development have left their mark.

However, a recent decision, to establish a reserve, has been 'cobbled together' by a rather haphazard-seeming arrangement between the private owners and the local authorities. From a visiting birder's viewpoint, the problem at El Hondo is one of finding a vantage point. By applying to the Conselleria de Medio ambiente, in Alicante, (telephone No. 96-592-24-11) a permit to visit may be obtained, when it is then possible to enter accompanied by the main gate at the northwest corner (incidentally, the big Cattle Egret roost is nearby) and proceed across the marsh to a raised observation point, from where there is a commanding view of the whole reserve. This may only be possible on certain days, and it is likely that the visitor will want to make other visits to the area.

A good way to get the flavour of El Hondo is to take the left turn from the La Marina — Elche road to Los Perez, where you go straight across a fast main road (San Fulgencio-

Elche) between 2 reservoirs. Immediately, on the right, you pass an area of wasteland where Pratincole have bred in recent years, then some good little muddy pools before coming alongside some very tall reeds. These can only be overlooked by climbing on top of your car, but you are now in the area where White-headed Duck first bred after an absence of many years, and where Marbled Duck also breed.

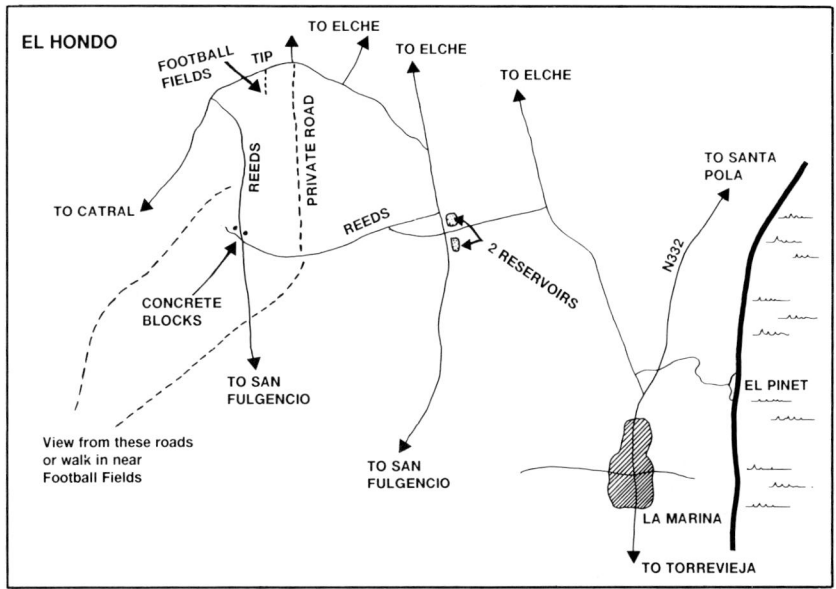

This area is particularly good in winter, with raptors everywhere, Bluethroat, Moustached Warbler and Penduline Tit in the reedbeds and egrets and herons in abundance.

Further on, it is possible to take a right turn, over a king-sized speed-bump and follow a quiet road, from which most of the local specialities can be watched. Some way along, a metal bridge crosses an irrigation ditch, and provides welcome elevation. Another Pratincole colony has been found close by.

There are many other good spots in the region south of Elche, and patient exploration should pay off. One such is the small wetland of El Hondo de Amoros, near San Fulgencio, best pinpointed by leaving the huge sprawl of the La Marina Urbanisation by way of 'Oasis', and seeing the marsh from slightly higher ground. This is a good spot for Marbled Duck, herons and other species.

10. SIERRA DE CREVILLENTE (map ref. R27)

This is a small but remarkably interesting area of craggy mountains, with some fine, spectacular, cliffs, approached through the very ordinary town of Crevillente, on the old main road from Elche to Murcia. Simply drive up into the town to the right of the main road, and find a palm-filled ravine that splits the old town. Keep to the right of this and follow the road out into the Sierra. A short gorge is left by means of a sharp right turn under an old aqueduct, then the narrow road meanders up past some sensational crags. Raptors have been seen in some variety here, and there are populations of Alpine Swift, Bee-Eater, Black Wheatear, Crag Martin, etc. Trumpeter Finch has been reported from this area.

11. LA MATA/TORREVIEJA (map ref. R27 & S27)

The two great salt-lagoons of the south of the Province are not at all easy to approach. La Mata, the northernmost, is, however, the most accessible, and a rough track runs right along the southern shore. From here, waders may often be found near the western end, where a narrow spit runs out into the lake. At this point, there is also a reedbed, holding a few pairs of warblers. The scrub along the shore is good for shrikes.

The bigger Torrevieja lake is surrounded by private land for much of its circumference, but there are places where you can walk down to it, and, indeed, across it. The difficulty is one of seeing anything over the vast expanse of water, but the best approach is from the A341 road to the east of Montesinos, where a road leads to a causeway over the lake.

12. SAN MIGUEL DE SALINAS (map ref. S27)

Most Northern European birders would be interested in the fact that Red-necked Nightjar is a regular breeding species near San Miguel. In mid-summer, simply wait until dusk, then drive out of San Miguel to the south and take the turning for Rebate. At the 3km post, up near the top of the hill, you should hear the characteristic call. Also in the area are Stone Curlew and several Bee-Eater colonies, as well as the odd pair of Buzzards.

The nearby Embalse de la Pedrera is crossed by a road-causeway, and is generally birdless, though the arid hillsides are good for Stone Curlew, larks and wheatears, and Red-rumped Swallow may be found nearby.

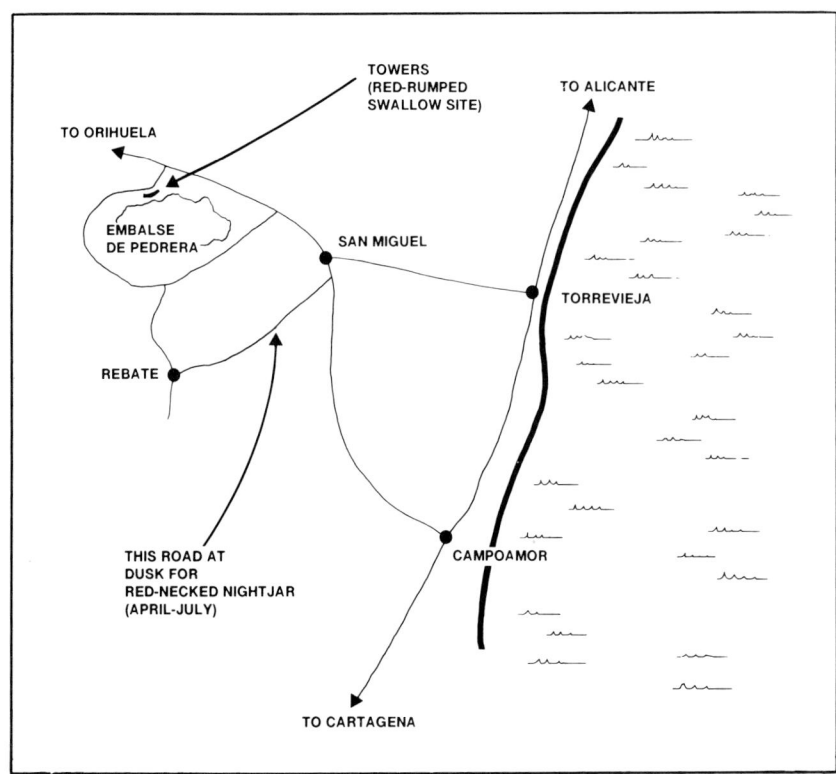

20

It must be stressed that the above is only a selection of SOME of the best sites in Alicante Province, and there are many more spots where birds may be seen as well as, or better than, those described. The northern extremities of the Province, bordering on Valencia and Albacete, have interesting points, such as the remnant 'steppes' near Villena, and there are places in other parts of the region which look inviting. One such is the saline lagoon shown on the map, appropriately enough, at Salinas, near Elda. This turns out to be a dried-up salt-flat, at least in summer, with little to be seen.

There are also some promising-looking crags, in many parts of the Province. The road from Albatera, near Crevillente, to Hondon de los Frailes, crosses a rocky pass, which looks as if it should hold the odd pair of raptors. So far, however, the author has discovered little of note in this area, though this does not, of course, mean that there IS nothing . . .

In short, there is still a lot of work to be done, on breeding species, and on migrants, before the bird populations of this sunny corner of Spain can be fully understood.

SYSTEMATIC LIST

Red-throated Diver *Gavia stellata*
One was reported off Torrevieja in November 1990.

Great Northern Diver *Gavia immer*
The only record of this species in the Province is of two birds at the Playa de Saladar, near Alicante, in January 1990, though there have been sightings a little further north, around Valencia, in the past.

Little Grebe *Tachybaptus ruficollis*
Present throughout the year in suitable habitat, with many pairs present on El Hondo, and a probable autumn influx, with some very impressive winter flocks.

Great Crested Grebe *Podiceps cristatus*
Good winter numbers, both on the sea and fresh water, 30 pairs reported breeding at El Hondo in 1985. More recently, some 12 pairs were counted at Santa Pola in 1991.

Black-necked Grebe *Podiceps nigricollis*
Little parties frequent in winter and spring. Recently rediscovered as a scarce breeding species at El Hondo. In April 1993, a leucistic bird was a strange sight at that location.

Cory's Shearwater *Calonectris diomedea*
Good numbers occur in spring and autumn, especially in windy weather. May breed on rocky islets in one or two places. In winter, may also be seen, but usually in much smaller numbers than at passage times, and often far out at sea.

Mediterranean Shearwater *Puffinus mauretanicus*
Abundant off-shore, especially in winter. Like the last species, may breed on a few islets. The systematics of this and the closely-related Manx *P.puffinus* have been the subject of much debate, and it may be that more than one race — and even more than one species — occurs.

Storm Petrel *Hydrobates pelagicus*
Breeds on the islet off Benidorm Island, and probably the rocky stack off Tabarca. Numbers at the former site appear to fluctuate, with a minimum of 150 pairs found in 1989, but no more than 20 pairs recorded the following year.

Gannet *Sula bassana*
Big numbers fish off Tabarca in the winter, especially when windy. Many more pass further out to sea. The closely-related Cape Gannet *S.capensis* has been recorded elsewhere on the Mediterranean coast in recent springs, and should be watched for off the Alicante coast. Even more exciting was a record of Masked Booby *Sula dactylatra* a few kilometres to the north, off Valencia, in March 1989.

Cormorant *Phalacrocorax carbo*
Many on the salinas in the winter months, with flocks of 40 not uncommon, and total numbers at Santa Pola often well in excess of 100 birds.

Shag *Phalacrocorax aristotelis*
May possibly breed on rocky coastlines, although scope may now be limited, and only regularly recorded at Benidorm Island, where records usually refer to juveniles in autumn. There is a record of three at El Hondo in 1972, but no recent inland records.

Bittern *Botaurus stellaris*
A very scarce passage migrant. There were several records of a single bird in 1991, from Santa Pola and from Pego, which may have all referred to one individual.

Little Bittern *Ixobrychus minutus*
An abundant summer visitor to the reedbeds, when its presence is often detected from its distinctive call. A male at El Hondo in early March 1992 was very early, but another at Santa Pola almost exactly a year later seems to indicate a small but regular early arrival. Another possibility is that a few birds winter from time to time. Breeding numbers are difficult to estimate, but 1991 censuses recorded 105 pairs on El Hondo, 60-80 pairs at Pego, and 10-15 at Santa Pola.

Night Heron *Nycticorax nycticorax*
Principally a migrant, but around 40-50 pairs breed at El Hondo, in a reedbed location which they share with Cattle Egrets *Bubulcus ibis,* and maybe elsewhere.

Squacco Heron *Ardeola ralloides*
A rare breeding visitor, largely to El Hondo, where a maximum of 30 pairs was recorded in 1977. More recently reduced to less than half that number, and always more likely to be met with as a scarce migrant, often turning up in late April. Present well into October in some years.

Cattle Egret *Bubulcus ibis*
One of the success stories of recent years, with a small flock of about 4 individuals in the mid-eighties growing to a substantial colony, with around 450 pairs breeding in reedbeds on El Hondo by 1993. Another flock may be found around Pego, and this also seems to be on the increase, though breeding has not so far been monitored. They do seem to travel around widely to feed, and the absence of livestock means that tractors may be adopted as surrogate cows!

Great White Egret *Egretta alba*
A few recent records, of occasional vagrants, give hope that, as in the Camargue, this welcome visitor may become a more regular feature. A few May sightings at scattered localities may be of less significance than the record of one at Santa Pola for 11 days in January 1991.

Little Egret *Egretta garzetta*
Perhaps one of the most characteristic birds of the wetlands of the Province, with some very large flocks, especially at Santa Pola in the spring. Breeding numbers are estimated at something like 200 pairs at El Hondo.

Grey Heron *Ardea cinerea*
A breeding species, in increasing numbers, with a very big influx in September. Wintering birds seem to remain well into March, and have some very large gatherings.

Purple Heron *Ardea purpurea*
A common summer visitor, with, however, perhaps less than 100 pairs, and a short season, a few lingering until late September, or even into October, as evidence a singleton at Pego on 12 October 1993. Breeding recorded at Pego, Santa Pola and El Hondo.

Black Stork *Ciconia nigra*
Recorded annually between 1989 and 1993, with singletons seen between September and December, and is almost certainly of regular annual occurrence.

White Stork *Ciconia ciconia*
Small flocks are recorded at migration times at widely-separated localities, but probably under-recorded, and always likely at passage times, when flocks probably pass over at a considerable height.

Glossy Ibis *Plegadis falcinellus*
Until 1992, was simply an occasional vagrant. In that summer, however, a group of seven appeared in the spring at El Hondo. Breeding success, if any, is unknown. A single bird in

May 1993 gave rise to hopes once again, especially when further sightings were recorded throughout the summer.

Spoonbill *Platalea leucorodia*
Small numbers are regularly recorded wintering on the Salinas of Santa Pola, but this species remains a rarity in the area. Two adults were at Pego on 12 October 1993.

Greater Flamingo *Phoenicopterus ruber*
Has bred historically on the salinas of Santa Pola, and may do so again if a proper reserve could be established. The same applies at El Hondo, where breeding was last attempted in 1965. Still regularly present, with flocks of up to 1,000 birds not unusual. Colour rings from Fuente Piedra (Granada) are commonly seen, and a number of birds ringed in the Rhone Delta are also seen. Upwards of 2,000 were present during the winter of 1992/3, when mysterious deaths occurred on El Hondo, which were put down to high levels of lead pollution following hunting.

Lesser Flamingo *Phoenicopterus minor*
One was found at El Hondo in mid-September, 1993, and any records in this southerly part of Europe should be regarded as at least 'possible' wild individuals.

Greylag Goose *Anser anser*
A regular winter visitor to El Hondo, where flocks of up to 30 may be seen.

Ruddy Shelduck *Tadorna ferruginea*
A single adult present on Santa Pola salinas in the autumn of 1993 may have been a wild bird, though this is, of course, impossible to verify.

Shelduck *Tadorna tadorna*
First appeared as a breeding species at El Hondo in 1983, and appears to be in the process of colonisation, breeding around La Mata, and probably in the neighbourhood of the salinas at Santa Pola, where winter influxes are regular, in small numbers.

Wigeon *Anas penelope*
A numerous winter visitor, much hunted, like all wildfowl in the province. In late January 1993, a flock of 360 birds was present on lagoons to the north of El Hondo.

Gadwall *Anas strepera*
A scarce and irregular breeding species at El Hondo, also a migrant and winter visitor, with 45 birds counted in January 1991.

Teal *Anas crecca*
A sparingly distributed passage migrant (more regular in autumn than in spring) and winter visitor, apt to fluctuate wildly in numbers, with 527 counted at El Hondo in November 1989, and scarcely any the following year.

Mallard *Anas platyrhynchos*
Present at all times, with a breeding population of around 100 pairs at El Hondo. Also breeeds at Pego and on the salinas of Santa Pola.

Pintail *Anas acuta*
An erratic winter visitor, with 1,000 recorded at El Hondo in February 1974, some 400 at Santa Pola in January 1989, and 480 in January 1993.

Garganey *Anas querquedula*
Occurs sparingly and mainly as a spring migrant, often in pairs, though now and again, good-sized flocks occur in March, often at Santa Pola (maximum recorded — 23 at the Clot de Galvany in March 1990). Appears to have been an occasional breeding species at El Hondo, and may still be.

Shoveler *Anas clypeata*
An abundant winter visitor to suitable waters, starting to arrive in September, and staying well into April. A count of 3,600 birds at El Hondo in January 1991 was probably not exceptional. Summer records are not unknown — may breed.

Marbled Duck *Marmaronetta angustirostris*
A shy and retiring, but quite well-established breeding bird of El Hondo and the salinas of Santa Pola, where it may be increasing, though the species was certainly more numerous before recent habitat-loss, and a flock of 400 was counted at El Hondo in October 1973. A recent estimate is that perhaps 15-20 pairs are breeding. This species largely departs in mid-winter, returning in February to its breeding haunts. Breeding has also been suspected at the Clot de Galvany, and, in recent years, at Pego, where 16 individuals were counted in September 1993.

Red-crested Pochard *Netta rufina*
The breeding population in the Elche area probably numbers around 200 pairs, and big arrivals in autumn can lead to winter flocks of over 1,000, and sometimes many more. Breeding also occurs at Pego, where a recent survey put the population at 15-20 pairs.

Pochard *Aythya ferina*
As a breeding bird, less numerous than the last species, but can run to huge flocks in the winter months, with flocks running into four figures on many suitable waters. Breeding numbers were recently put at some 60 pairs.

Ferruginous Duck *Aythya nyroca*
In recent years, has simply been found as a rare vagrant, usually in winter, but a female with eight chicks was seen on the Clot de Galvany in July 1990, giving rise to hopes of re-establishment of this rare species.

Tufted Duck *Aythya fuligula*
A scarce and irregular winter visitor, usually amongst Coot *Fulica atra* flocks. Small flocks of up to 12 birds were at El Hondo in January 1993, whilst a census in 1991 put the winter population there at 30 birds.

Common Scoter *Melanitta nigra*
Small flocks are seen offshore in the winter months, usually between December and February.

Red-breasted Merganser *Mergus serrator*
Very occasionally, this northern species turns up along the coastline in the winter months, even more occasionally being seen on salt-lagoons.

Ruddy Duck *Oxyura jamaicensis*
See next species.

White-headed Duck *Oxyura leucocephala*
Although there is a record of one bird shot in December 1959, there is little evidence that this species was historically common, but a dramatic turn of events was provided when two pairs bred successfully at El Hondo in 1991, raising 9 and 6 young respectively. There are concerns regarding the purity of the population following reports of hybridization elsewhere with the closely-related Ruddy Duck *O. jamaicensis,* and hybrids have already been shot as have at least three examples of *O. jamaicensis* (May 1993). Urgent measures are in hand, but whilst the unwelcome American intruders are still being encouraged outside Spanish borders, the threat to a beautiful and rare species is bound to remain. There remains, of course, the contention that, if they are, indeed, specifically distinct, interbreeding will present no ultimate threat. Rare away from the breeding areas, but there is a record of an immature bird on the sea off Santa Pola in November 1991.

Honey Buzzard *Pernis apivorus*
There are a few May, June and September records, usually of small migrant flocks, and the species probably passes over regularly on spring passage. Two birds were seen at El Hondo in December 1989.

Black Kite *Milvus migrans*
Records of odd birds overflying the area are usually in spring (March/April), or autumn (September/October), with an annual average of two sightings in recent years.

Red Kite *Milvus milvus*
A wanderer was seen over El Hondo in May 1972. Another was found roosting in the town of Denia in May 1990.

Griffon Vulture *Gyps fulvus*
Several winter records exist, and an extraordinary sequence of sightings refers to a group of 50 in the Sierra de Cravillente in late October 1989, with a further party of 70 there a week later. Two were captured, in Guardamar and Santa Pola, in October and December respectively of 1991 — by what means is unclear! There is also a record of one resting on a rooftop in Santa Pola in October of the previous year, so there may be a small but regular passage along the coast in late autumn.

Short-toed Eagle *Circaetus gallicus*
A&G mention a 'breeding population' in the northwest of the province, but this appears to require confirmation. Occurs fairly frequently as a migrant, and one remained at the Cabo de Santa Pola during much of August, 1989.

Marsh Harrier *Circus aeruginosus*
Certainly bred in the relatively recent past, but probably does so no longer, almost undoubtedly due to disturbance. Abundant outside the breeding season, with possibly upwards of 30 individuals in the Elche/Santa Pola area.

Hen Harrier *Circus cyaneus*
A scarce, though probably regular, winter visitor, with 'ringtails' providing the majority of the sightings, usually in singles.

Montagu's Harrier *Circus pygargus*
Appears to be mainly a spring migrant, though may breed occasionally. Up to seven birds have been seen together at Santa Pola. A melanistic bird was at Santa Pola in September 1991.

Goshawk *Accipiter gentilis*
Occasional on the wetlands in the winter months and present in very small numbers as a breeding bird in the high pinewoods.

Sparrowhawk *Accipiter nisus*
Much as the last species.

Buzzard *Buteo buteo*
Not at all uncommon in the lowlands in winter, but surprisingly scarce as a breeding bird, with a pair defending territory near San Miguel de Salinas in July 1990 the only recent record.

Spotted Eagle *Aquila clanga*
Two (possibly three) were present in December 1989 at El Hondo, one of which was still in the area the following March. There are no previous records, but regular occurrence in the Rhone delta suggests that this is another under-recorded species. At least two were also present during the early part of 1993, certainly including one adult.

Imperial Eagle *Aquila heliaca*
An adult of the Spanish race *A.h. adelberti* was seen going to roost at El Hondo in January 1993. This is well outside the species' normal range, and wandering far from breeding grounds is not normal for this race, but there may be some connection with the unusually dry conditions that winter.

Golden Eagle *Aquila chrysaetos*
The latest estimate is that there are around four pairs breeding, all in the northern Sierras, and certainly birds are seen frequently in the Maigmó area.

Booted Eagle *Hieraaetus pennatus*
There are two December records from El Hondo, in 1980 and 1983, which is unexpected, and other recent sightings are, more typically, of single birds, heading northwards in March, and of two over Elche in September 1991. At least three birds appear to have wintered around El Hondo in 1992/3.

Bonelli's Eagle *Hieraaetus fasciatus*
This species is not often met with in the Province during the breeding season, but there are records from the northern mountains, and, more recently, from the Sierra de Crevillente, where a pair was seen, in ideal breeding habitat, in June 1993. Three immatures soared over El Hondo in January 1993, and there have been other winter records, from widely scattered parts of the region.

Osprey *Pandion haliaetus*
One winters regularly on the Salinas de Bonmati, Santa Pola, and the species is recorded as of regular winter occurrence at El Hondo. The species is normally absent from April to September.

Lesser Kestrel *Falco naumanni*
Has bred in the Province, but more normally occurs as a rare vagrant, with recent records including one at the Embalse de Pedrera in July 1991, and one at the Cabo de Santa Pola in October of the same year.

Kestrel *Falco tinnunculus*
A resident in small numbers all around the Province.

Merlin *Falco columbarius*
Not at all uncommon in the winter months, especially in the wetlands.

Hobby *Falco subbuteo*
A scarce migrant, in spring or autumn, October being the best month.

Eleonora's Falcon *Falco eleonorae*
One took up all too brief residence on a balcony overlooking Santa Pola harbour in November 1991, clearly believing it to be a sea-cliff! The bird was seen well, by an experienced observer, and was an adult male.

Peregrine *Falco peregrinus*
There are several records in most years of passage, or wintering birds, but the small breeding population is restricted to the northernmost parts of the Province. Pairs probably breed in the Jalón area, and birds are regularly reported around the Penon de Ifach, where there are plenty of suitable sites for nesting. Not infrequently found wintering around the wetland areas.

Red-legged Partridge *Alectoris rufa*
Common throughout the drier areas of the Province.

Quail *Coturnix coturnix*
Commonly heard throughout the cultivated lowlands, staying from March through to

September. A bird near La Marina in January 1993 may well have been over-wintering.

Water Rail *Rallus aquaticus*
Plentiful throughout the year in reedbeds.

Spotted Crake *Porzana porzana*
Such records as there are of this 'difficult' species are concentrated in spring, with April birds from 1982 and 1986, and two separate sightings — one each from Santa Pola and El Hondo — in March 1992.

Little Crake *Porzana parva*
Again, such records as can be traced suggest spring migration.

Baillon's Crake *Porzana pusilla*
Another species whose status is uncertain, but N-M thinks that 'breeding cannot be discounted' at El Hondo.

Corncrake *Crex crex*
There are two records (November 1991, December 1972) from the Salinas de Santa Pola, and one (September 1973) from El Hondo. It is likely, then, that this species is no more than a rare vagrant, but, due to its secretive nature, there is the possibility that it is a winter visitor.

Moorhen *Gallinula chloropus*
Abundant in suitable places. The only population-estimate is of 600-700 pairs at El Hondo.

Coot *Fulica atra*
Abundant in the wetlands, with some huge winter flocks. The highest count on record is of 12,000 at El Hondo in October 1973, but the number at Santa Pola may well exceed this in some years. Peak numbers seem to occur in the early part of the winter (October-January).

Crested Coot *Fulica cristata*
There are 2 unconfirmed records, both from April 1985, at El Hondo, but this species is always to be looked out for amongst the flocks of *F.atra*.

Crane *Grus grus*
There are a few records of singletons, mainly in March or November, but four birds wintered around El Hondo in 1992/3, and in early March 1993, a flock of 23 was seen flying west over El Hondo just before sunset. May well be under-recorded.

Oystercatcher *Haematopus ostralegus*
Winter visitor (rarely) and passage bird in small numbers.

Black-winged Stilt *Himantopus himantopus*
A common breeding species, especially at Santa Pola and El Hondo, where the population was estimated at 100 pairs in 1985. The tendency of this species to overwinter may be increasing, though it does show a tendency to disappear during rare spells of hard weather.

Avocet *Recurvirostra avosetta*
Very numerous as a breeding resident at Santa Pola, where perhaps 500 pairs nest. Numbers are augmented in winter, and flocks of upwards of 1,500 birds have been counted.

Stone Curlew *Burhinus oedicnemus*
A common bird in the dry hills around San Miguel de Salinas, and around the Torrevieja area. Maximum counts of 60 birds have been encountered at La Mata. The species' status outside the breeding season is not well known, but a nestling ringed in Norfolk, England

was shot at Santa Pola in November 1990. Certainly also present on the salt-flats around Villena, and probably at many other suitable locations.

Collared Pratincole *Glareola pratincola*
A species with a tendency to increase its breeding population in recent years, and the 1990 population at El Hondo may have been as high as 60 pairs, in two distinct colonies. The marginal land favoured as breeding grounds, however, give rise for concern for this bird's future, and habitat-loss could yet threaten its presence as a breeding species. Used to breed at Pego in the north of the Province, though this may not now occur, again due to changes in land-use. Three birds on 3rd April, 1993, at El Hondo, were uncharacteristically early, the majority of the birds tending to arrive at the end of that month, most having gone by the end of August.

Little Ringed Plover *Charadrius dubius*
Breeding occurs, though probably irregularly, at suitable waters, such as the Embalse de Pedrera and at Pego. Otherwise a scarce passage migrant, with a few winter records.

Ringed Plover *Charadrius hiaticula*
A regular migrant, usually in small numbers, and also present in winter.

Kentish Plover *Charadrius alexandrinus*
A common resident of the dry margins of salinas and undisturbed beaches. It is probable that the breeding population of the Province is in excess of 1,000 pairs.

Golden Plover *Pluvialis apricaria*
Uncommon but regular as a winter visitor to the lowlands around the southern side of El Hondo, where as many as 50 birds have been counted, and more particularly, to the Salinas de Torrevieja, where 150 were counted in January 1991.

Grey Plover *Pluvialis squaterola*
Quite numerous at Santa Pola and other coastal wetlands, especially on autumn passage, but also in smaller numbers in winter.

Lapwing *Vanellus vanellus*
A regular winter visitor, with flocks as large as 500 recorded at El Hondo, but usually in much smaller groups.

Knot *Calidris canutus*
An irregular passage migrant, usually occurring in small flocks, often in May.

Sanderling *Calidris alba*
Not uncommon on the quieter sandy beaches, and on salinas, from August to April, wintering birds at La Mata may number 40-50 most years.

Little Stint *Calidris minuta*
Numerous in winter, as well as on both passages. Counts of well over 100 are not unusual at Santa Pola, and all other suitable wetlands are well-populated, particularly from December through to February.

Temminck's Stint *Calidris temminckii*
In September 1991, an artificial pond was created at Guardamar, and this quickly attracted the first flock reliably recorded in the Province (though it is quite possible that the species has been overlooked in the past) of 11 birds, which stayed in the area, also visiting the Salinas de Santa Pola, until at least December. A single bird was also seen in September 1992, at El Hondo, and a flock of five was at Guardamar in April, 1993.

Pectoral Sandpiper *Calidris melanotos*
A first-year bird was observed at Santa Pola in April 1991, constituting the first spring record for Iberia.

Curlew Sandpiper *Calidris ferruginea*
Big flocks can be seen at Santa Pola in spring and autumn, often as many as 60-strong. The maximum census-count at Santa Pola is one of 462 birds, in August, 1989. Regular in spring and autumn at all other suitable wetlands.

Purple Sandpiper *Calidris maritima*
One spent several weeks at Cabo Cervera during the winter of 1991/2.

Dunlin *Calidris alpina*
Common in winter, when big flocks may build up at El Hondo, and on the salinas. The best numbers tend to be in January.

Ruff *Philomachus pugnax*
Most common in spring, when flocks of 40 or more birds are frequent at Santa Pola, but may be met with at almost any time of the year.

Snipe *Gallinago gallinago*
A sparingly represented winter visitor, sometimes staying into May, and returning in September.

Woodcock *Scolopax rusticola*
Occasional winter visitor, most frequently around the irrigation canals of the lowlands. Years frequently pass without a single record, however.

Black-tailed Godwit *Limosa limosa*
Huge numbers can be seen at Santa Pola in winter and on passage, with a maximum count of 2,000 at Bonmati alone in recent years, whilst the highest number recorded at El Hondo is 400. Non-breeders occasionally summer, but numbers are much reduced by early April.

Bar-tailed Godwit *Limosa lapponica*
Much scarcer than the last species, but more numerous in autumn than in spring, and usually to be found at Santa Pola, especially in September-October.

Whimbrel *Numenius phaeopus*
A passage migrant, often on rocky headlands and islands. One or two may overwinter on the coasts.

Curlew *Numenius arquata*
Never very numerous, but occurs regularly in winter and on passage, usually in small groups.

Spotted Redshank *Tringa erythropus*
A passage migrant and winter visitor, most common in April, with a high count of 700 birds at El Hondo, but more often in ones and twos. Some fine examples in breeding plumage are often to be found in spring.

Redshank *Tringa totanus*
Has bred at Santa Pola, and may do so elsewhere, but very plentiful as a migrant and winter visitor to all suitable areas.

Marsh Sandpiper *Tringa stagnatilis*
In recent years, has proved to be annual in the region, with singles regularly seen at Santa Pola. A group of five, seen there in April, 1991, was unusual. Return passage is usually in July and August.

Greenshank *Tringa nebularia*
A common migrant on both passages, and winter resident in suitable areas, though seldom in more than ones and twos.

Green Sandpiper *Tringa ochropus*
A passage migrant and winter visitor in small numbers, often to be found in the irrigation ditches and channels of the lowlands.

Wood Sandpiper *Tringa galreola*
A regular visitor on both passages, possibly more frequent in spring, when April is the peak time, and flocks of 10-20 are not uncommon. Return migration may start as early as the first week of July.

Common Sandpiper *Actitis hypoleucos*
Present at all times at suitable sites, with a peak at spring passage-time, but may well be found to breed, possibly at El Hondo.

Turnstone *Arenaria interpres*
A migrant, generally in small numbers, and probably most common on autumn passage. Also winters in southern coastal areas, where flocks of 20-30 have been counted.

Wilson's Phalarope *Phalaropus tricolor*
An adult female on 1st May 1987 was the fourth record for Spain and was watched for some time at Bonmati salinas, Santa Pola.

Red-necked Phalarope *Phalaropus lobatus*
Two in December 1989, and a further two which stayed from July into August, 1991, were all at Santa Pola. May well be found to occur regularly on passage.

Grey Phalarope *Phalaropus fulicarius*
One at Salinas de Santa Pola in May 1991, and another in August 1992, are the only sightings on record.

Arctic Skua *Stercorarius parasiticus*
Surprisingly numerous off-shore in the winter months, when the considerable shoals of fish often attract good gatherings to the shore off El Pinet and La marina.

Great Skua *Stercorarius skua*
Ones and twos are seen in some winters off the coasts, often from the beach of El Pinet.

Mediterranean Gull *Larus melanocephalus*
Generally scarce, but there is some evidence of post-breeding gatherings being regular at Santa Pola with a best count of 7 there in August 1989. Groups of 15 and 16 have been recorded in recent years, at Villajoyosa, and at Cabo Cervera.

Laughing Gull *Larus atricilla*
A second winter bird was found at Salinas de Bonmati (coincidentally within 50 metres of the location of the Wilson's Phalarope *P. tricolor*!) on 13 October 1993, and described and photographed. This was after a series of westerly winds which brought much bad weather to the rest of Europe, but spared Alicante.

Little Gull *Larus minutus*
Up to 20 birds have been feeding at the Salinas de Bonmati, Santa Pola, in recent springs, but not normally to be found at other seasons.

Black-headed Gull *Larus ridibundus*
Breeds in at least one large colony at Santa Pola (112 pairs — 1991), and is always abundant at suitable spots around the province, with some huge winter flocks, often of several thousand.

Slender-billed Gull *Larus genei*
May be on the increase, and breeding has now been proved, with at least one pair at Santa Pola in 1991. Wintering birds can be quite numerous, and up to 54 have been counted at Bonmati in winter.

Audouin's Gull *Larus audouini*
A large post-breeding flock roosting at Santa Pola had increased to around 580 individuals in August 1991, and other, smaller flocks may be found at Calpe (7-12) and near El Pinet. The species probably breeds on offshore islets, such as the ones off Tabarca, where birds are always to be seen in spring. Good winter numbers are regularly counted at the salt-lakes of Torrevieja and La Mata.

Common Gull *Larus canus*
One was at Alicante in March 1989. This is the sole record to hand.

Lesser Black-backed Gull *Larus fuscus*
A common winter visitor to all coasts, appearing in September and staying to April at least.

Herring Gull *Larus argentatus (cachinnans)*
Abundant on all coasts,. Breeding is recorded at Javea, Calpe and Benidorm Island, as well as at Santa Pola.

Iceland Gull *Larus glaucoides*
There is an old record of one bird in the Santa Pola area, 'in the early eighties', and clearly always a chance of a wanderer in the winter months.

Great Black-backed Gull *Larus marinus*
A very scarce winter visitor. Two occurred at Santa Pola in 1991. One, on the salinas, in February, and another, in the harbour, in September. In 1993, a bird on the salinas, near Santa Pola, was present on the extremely early date of 28th August.

Kittiwake *Rissa tridactyla*
There are occasional winter records of this northern species, usually from the rocky headlands. Denia and Cabo Cervera have been most favoured in recent years.

Gull-billed Tern *Gelochelidon nilotica*
N-M refers to a small breeding colony at Torrevieja, and certainly there were two individuals nearby in April 1986, but whether they are still breeding there in the face of unchecked 'development' is unclear. Otherwise, a scarce wanderer, tending to appear in June and July.

Caspian Tern *Sterna caspia*
Seems to be becoming more regular, with the first record, of one at El Hondo in September 1985, being followed by a welter of sightings since 1989, many referring to more than one bird, always in the neighbourhood of Santa Pola, with a tendency towards March and September as the favourite months, and certainly now annual. An adult at Pego in early July, 1993, was unexpected.

Royal Tern *Sterna maxima*
A record of one at Santa Pola, in September 1991, awaits confirmation. Certainly a bird to be looked out for.

Lesser Crested Tern *Sterna bengalensis*
One was with Sandwich Terns *S. sandvicensis* at Cabo Cervera in January, 1991. Undoubtedly a bird which could be recorded with some frequency in the Province, were there more observers.

Sandwich Tern *Sterna sandvicensis*
A migrant and winter resident, particularly at El Pinet/Bonmati, where there is a regular roost on salinas, and where birds fish offshore at most seasons. Also present in summer in the area, but breeding information is not available.

Alhama, the flat "steppe" country to the south of Murcia near to the small town of Alhama has a small population of Black-bellied Sandgrouse as well as Calandra Larks, Short-toed and Lesser Short-toed Larks. Other species typical of the area are Stone Curlew, Montagu's Harrier and Roller.

The extensive area collectively known as El Hondo is criss-crossed by many tracks and provides opportunities to explore much of this bird rich area.

Island of Tabarca, looking towards the eastern end of the island with its disused lighthouse in the distance. The whole area is good for migrant birds, especially in the spring.

El Hondo.

Common Tern *Sterna hirundo*
A very numerous passage migrant, with a colony at Santa Pola, where perhaps 200 pairs breed, returning from its southern wintering areas in early April. Breeding also occurs at La Mata and Torrevieja salt-lakes.

Arctic Tern *Sterna paradisaea*
One, with Sandwich Terns *S. sandvicensis,* was seen at Santa Pola on 30th September 1990. Probably overlooked at times.

Little Tern *Sterna albifrons*
46 pairs were breeding at El Hondo in 1991, when they were last counted, and there were more than 250 pairs at Santa Pola. Further colonies exist at La Mata, Torrevieja, and Pedrera, with a few pairs at Pego and the Clot de Galvany. Summer residents, from April to September.

Whiskered Tern *Chlidonias hybrida*
A breeding population of perhaps 200 pairs withstands the encroachment of agriculture and other pressures around El Hondo and at Santa Pola, and this is a species which would undoubtedly thrive on further protection. Occasionally to be found wintering in very small numbers, and back in strength by late March.

Black Tern *Chlidonias niger*
A passage migrant, seen more often in spring than in autumn (when it is possible that many are overlooked), and also an occasional breeder.

White-winged Black Tern *Chlidonias leucopterus*
There is an August record, of a bird at Pego, otherwise, all sightings are of May birds, usually in ones and twos, in the southern wetlands.

Razorbill *Alca torda*
A surprisingly common winter visitor to in-shore waters, in some years, but absent in others, 65 birds were off Cabo Roig, in December 1989.

Black-bellied Sandgrouse *Pterocles orientalis*
A small, sedentary flock is to be found in *salicornia* steppe, near to the town of Villena. They probably number no more than 20 individuals, and are undoubtedly a relic of a once-healthy population, now threatened by agricultural encroachment on their specialised habitat.

Rock Dove *Columba livia*
Resident in suitable coastal localities. Apparently pure-bred birds may be found on offshore islands.

Stock Dove *Columba oenas*
Mentioned in A&G as a local breeding species, but requires confirmation.

Woodpigeon *Columba palumbus*
A scarce resident, most likely to be met with in the wooded areas to the south, and passage migrant. A party of 60 which appeared at Pego in October 1993 was unusual.

Collared Dove *Streptopelia decaocto*
May well be in the process of colonization, with regular sightings around Elche in 1990, but apparently no records in 1991, followed by many sightings in 1993. It is worth mentioning that the similar *S.risoria*, an escape from captivity, is also at large in the area, so that caution should be observed.

Turtle Dove *Streptopelia turtur*
Common summer visitor and passage migrant, first appearing in mid-April.

Monk Parakeet *Myiopsitta monachus*
A few of these South American birds appear to have been liberated in the Province, and may turn up almost anywhere.

Ring-necked Parakeet *Psittacula krameri*
Two at Santa Pola in September 1991 were a strange sight. Presumably they would not find colonisation too difficult. One was also seen at Benidorm in December 1990.

Great Spotted Cuckoo *Clamator glandarius*
Occurs rarely on passage, but is only to be looked for as a breeding species where there are Magpies *Pica pica*. Parasitisation on that species occurs with some frequency at Villajoyosa.

Cuckoo *Cuculus canorus*
A common summer visitor, mainly to the wetlands, where the Reed Warbler *Acrocephalus scirpaceus* appears to be the favourite host species.

Barn Owl *Tyto alba*
As elsewhere, this species is most difficult to assess, but is certainly present at several localities, including the southern suburbs of Alicante city.

Scop's Owl *Otus scops*
Present as a breeding species in the Jalón valley, in the north of the Province, with several birds calling in most summers. Elsewhere, a scarce species, absent from some apparently suitable areas.

Eagle Owl *Bubu bubo*
This is another whose nocturnal habits make for a difficult study, but A&G regard the species as 'regular', and lots of suitable habitat is to be found in the Sierras.

Little Owl *Athene noctua*
A very common species, occupying a variety of habitats, and especially numerous in the undulating southern woodlands.

Tawny Owl *Strix aluco*
Another owl which poses problems for would-be researchers, and certainly local, at best, in the Province. Recent records point to the presence of one or more pairs at Maigmó.

Long-eared Owl *Asio otus*
Mentioned by A&G as an occasional breeding species. The above comments as to lack of records again apply, with the only definite record to hand being of one at Castalla in January 1991.

Short-eared Owl *Asio flammeus*
Two records in March 1991, then one in December of that year, all at Santa Pola, are the most recent records. Even much further north, this species is irruptive in its habits.

Nightjar *Caprimulgus europaeus*
There is evidence of spring passage, with several May records from El Hondo, and a recent May sighting at Benidorm Island.

Red-necked Nightjar *Caprimulgus ruficollis*
Breeds, probably in reasonable numbers, around San Miguel de Salinas, inhabiting hilly, mature, pinewoods. May well occur in similar country which may be found in various parts of the province, but this requires further research, due to the inclination of this species to call only very late in the evening.

Swift *Apus apus*
Widespread and very common, but caution as to confusion with the next species, which

has an extended breeding season, should be exercised, especially with early and late records. Normally starts to appear in the first week of April, around three weeks after the next species.

Pallid Swift *Apus pallidus*
Present at widely-scattered breeding sites around the province from March into October. Appears to favour the older buildings, such as the castle at Castalla, and the old church on Tabarca.

Alpine Swift *Apus melba*
There is a small colony on steep crags in the Sierra de Crevillente, probably not more than five pairs being present in 1993. There may well be other colonies in the northern Sierras, but the species is probably more likely to be met with as a passage migrant, almost anywhere.

Kingfisher *Alcedo atthis*
Very common around the dykes and streams of the wetlands, especially in autumn and winter, and certainly breeds in suitable habitat, though sparingly. (Absent from El Hondo from early March to early July, 1991)

Bee-eater *Merops apiaster*
A locally common summer visitor and bird of passage. The best colonies are to be found around San Miguel de Salinas, and on the slopes of the Sierra above Albaterra, where the clay banks provide ideal nest-sites. Arrivals are normally from mid-April, but one flew over La Marina on 1st April, 1993.

Roller *Coracias garrulus*
Apparently once bred commonly, but now a scarce bird, possibly as a result of persecution, and may no longer breed. Common, however, a few kilometres to the south, in Murcia Province. Five records, of May migrants, are split between 1989, 1991 and 1993, all from the south of the region. This is rather later than their normal arrival-date in Murcia, and may well suggest non-breeding wanderers.

Hoopoe *Upopa epops*
Common at all seasons in the lowland areas, often breeding in the plentiful olives. Numbers are probably augmented by birds from further north in winter, when the population may be very high.

Wryneck *Jynx torquilla*
A&G mention breeding in the northeast of the province. Also a regular passage visitor, and probably winters regularly in the south.

Green Woodpecker *Picus viridis*
A widely distributed resident, occupying a variety of habitats.

Great Spotted Woodpecker *Dendrocopos major*
Mentioned by A&G as a breeding species, but appears to require confirmation.

Calandra Lark *Melanocorypha calandra*
A local species in the province, at best, and may be difficult to locate. Its preference for lowland salt-flats makes it a species worth looking for in the extreme north-west of the region. Is found marginally outside of the area, near Ontinyent.

Short-toed Lark *Calandrella brachydactyla*
A summer visitor to suitable areas, often rocky headlands and islands, for example the island of Tabarca, which has a thriving population.

Lesser Short-toed Lark *Calandrella rufescens*
Breeds on salt-flats around El Hondo, near Villena, and at Salinas. Any bird of this genus

outside the breeding season is likely to be this species, and suitable habitat abounds in the Santa Pola/Torrevieja area, so that it is certainly worth keeping an eye out for a species which is common just to the south, in the Almería and Murcia Provinces.

Crested Lark *Galerida cristata*
An abundant species throughout the Province, occupying a wide variety of habitat.

Thekla Lark *Galerida theklae*
Replaces the last species in the rockier areas, but more work needs doing to establish the precise range of this bird — a project made more exacting by the difficulty of separation in the field of the two closely-related forms.

Woodlark *Lululla arborea*
May be found in wooded mountains, such as at Maigmó, where a bird was in song in April 1993, and winter flocks have been recorded elsewhere. A flock of 25 was at Montesinos in November 1991.

Skylark *Alauda arvensis*
Good winter flocks may be seen in the cultivated areas of the southern part of the province, sometimes 100 or more birds together.

Sand Martin *Riparia riparia*
Breeds in several suitable places, as well as being an abundant passage-migrant. Occasionally winters on the Elche wetlands.

Crag Martin *Ptyonoprogne rupestris*
There are several colonies in the high Sierras, notably around Guadalest and Penaguila, but the wintering flocks at El Hondo and Santa Pola may number many thousands, and are an impressive sight when bad weather brings them low in search of insects.

Swallow *Hirundo rustica*
Common migrant and summer visitor. May occasionally reach vast numbers, with a count of some 50,000 recorded at El Hondo one early November. Early arrivals may start before the end of February, and there are occasional December records at the other end of the calendar. Birds showing characters of the Egyptian race *H.r.savignii* have been recorded in the area.

Red-rumped Swallow *Hirundo daurica*
An occupied nest was found near Relleu in August 1989, and birds were present in breeding territory near Guadalest in late summer in 1991, but it is not clear whether these are unusual records, or part of an increasing trend. The species is well-established a short distance to the south, in Murcia Province, and Red-rumped Swallows certainly pass through the region, having been recorded amongst flocks of the last species for many years.

House Martin *Delichons urbica*
An abundant summer resident and migrant, with a breeding season much longer than would be expected in more northerly parts of its range. Instances of overwintering in the wetlands have been recorded, and early arrivals may well occur by the end of February, especially on the coast.

Tawny Pipit *Anthus campestris*
May well pass through more regularly than the few records suggest. These tend to be restricted to one or two passage migrants in most years, at a variety of localities, April and September being the preferred months.

Tree Pipit *Anthus trivialis*
A passage migrant, in small numbers, usually on the coast. Again under-recorded, and to be sought as early as late February or early March.

Meadow Pipit *Anthus pratensis*
An abundant winter visitor, mostly between October and March.

Red-throated Pipit *Anthus cervinus*
There is an April, 1993, record of one bird at Pego, and this species may well be overlooked elsewhere.

Water Pipit *Anthus spinoletta*
A regular winter visitor to the wetland areas, usually solitary. In some winters can be almost as numerous as *A. pratensis* in favourable habitat, such as the margins of disused salinas.

Yellow Wagtail *Motacilla flava*
A very common summer resident, whose population is augmented by the big numbers of passage birds in spring and autumn. Only the Spanish race *M.f. iberiae* appears to nest, but in a species as systematically complex as this, it would be difficult to attempt an assessment of the subspecies visiting the Province. Arrives from the end of February in spring.

Grey Wagtail *Motacilla cinerea*
A sparse but regular winter visitor and migrant, most numerous in October. Breeds only a little further north, and may yet be found to do so by fast-running streams in the Province.

White Wagtail *Motacilla alba*
A very numerous resident at all times. In January 1989, a male of the race *M.a.yarellii* was seen near San Fulgencio.

Wren *Troglodytes troglodytes*
A very local breeding bird in the Sierras, only found very rarely in the lowlands, during the winter months, although there is a record of a pair feeding young at Denia in 1989.

Dunnock *Prunella modularis*
A rare species in the area, with recent records confined to five sightings in 1989. One was in January, the remainder between October and December, including one trapped at Raspeig.

Alpine Accentor *Prunella collaris*
A very occasional winter vagrant. Four were in the Sierra de Crevillente in November 1989.

Rufous Bush Robin *Cercotrichas galactotes*
Can be a shy and difficult species to find, and is therefore doubtless overlooked, but certainly breeding in new coniferous plantations at the Cabo de Santa Pola (some six pairs present in 1990, increasingly slightly in each year since) and probably more numerous in the valleys to the north, where arrival tends to be in May.

Robin *Erithacus rubecula*
A common winter visitor. One, at least, was in woodland near Gorga in July 1990, and it now appears likely that a few pairs breed in montane forest at various locations in the northern Sierras.

Nightingale *Luscinia megarhynchos*
Summer visitor and regular passage migrant, most often met with in April.

Bluethroat *Luscinia svecica*
A winter visitor, on a regular basis, to the reedbeds, particularly of Pego and El Hondo, where birds of the White-spotted race *L.s.cyanecula* have been heard in full song in mid-March. Numbers in reed-bed localities are difficult to assess, but there seems likely to be a sizeable population in most winters, arriving quite early, often by the end of September.

Black Redstart *Phoenicurus ochruros*
An abundant winter visitor, especially in coastal towns and gardens. Otherwise a breeding species in rocky places throughout the Province, in very small numbers. In April 1990, an albinistic bird in the Sierra de Crevillente was completely white, save for a pale pink tail.

Redstart *Phoenicurus phoenicurus*
A regular passage migrant, usually along the coast, and in small numbers. Early arrivals may occur from the first days of March.

Whinchat *Saxicola rubetra*
Again a passsage migrant often in good numbers in early spring particularly in April.

Stonechat *Saxicola torquata*
A very numerous resident in most parts of the Province, probably commonest in marginal agricultural situations.

Wheatear *Oenanthe oenanthe*
A common migrant, usually on the coast, appearing in early March, with return passage in September and October.

Black-eared Wheatear *Oenanthe hispanica*
A summer resident, especially on the rocky wastelands such as are found behind Torrevieja, and also a passage migrant, arriving from mid-March in spring, and sometimes appearing before the last species.

Black Wheatear *Oenanthe leucura*
A regular and common breeding species in ravines and sometimes in old buildings, almost invariably in coastal localities, or craggy mountains. Tends to wander outside the breeding season, when it may be met with in towns and new building estates.

Blue Rock Thrush *Monticola solitarius*
Often found in similar habitat to the last species, but also present in higher, mountainous country. Sedentary.

Rock Thrush *Monticola saxatilis*
One or two records appear to be the annual norm for this scarce migrant, with no discernible pattern, January, March, May and October all having had records in the last three years recorded.

Ring Ouzel *Turdus torquatus*
A group of nine birds, seen in the Sierra de Crevillente on an unspecified date in 1988 is the sole traceable record, but there is a chance that a few may winter in the high Sierras, as, indeed, they do some way south in the Sierra Nevada.

Blackbird *Turdus merula*
Not nearly so universal as in Northern Europe, but present and sedentary in a variety of wooded habitats throughout the area.

Fieldfare *Turdus pilaris*
One was seen at Monovar in January 1989. The Province is well to the south of the species' normal winter range.

Song Thrush *Turdus philomelos*
Winters, occasionally congregating in flocks of up to 60 birds, often in the valleys of the Sierras, but also in agricultural and wetland areas.

Redwing *Turdus iliacus*
A scarce winter visitor, usually in ones and twos, but flocks of 10 have been seen at El Hondo.

Mistle Thrush *Turdus pilaris*
A scarce and local resident, with a few pairs in the orchards and groves of the foothills of the Sierras.

Cetti's Warbler *Cettia cetti*
A common visitor to the larger wetland areas between September and March, and may remain to breed in some areas, but certainly appears to be absent from El Hondo in at least some summers.

Fan-tailed Warbler *Cisticola juncidis*
Resident, subject, as elsewhere in its range, to periodic fluctuations in population. Very often found in crops of alfalfa etc., and to be found in many parts of the province, especially when its song renders it so conspicuous during the spring.

Grasshopper Warbler *Locustella naevia*
A scarce migrant on both passages, probably overlooked more often than not, and most likely to be found at El Hondo or in similar reedbed locations.

Savi's Warbler *Locustella luscinioides*
A sparse breeding population exists at El Hondo, and possibly at other reedbed sites, but it is unlikely that the total number of breeding pairs exceeds ten.

Moustached Warbler *Acrocephalus melanopogon*
The precise status of this species is unclear, though it is, if anything, a rare breeding bird. Certainly present, however, for much of the year at Pego and El Hondo, and N-M records singing birds throughout winter. Only three singing males could be located at El Hondo in May 1991.

Sedge Warbler *Acrocephalus schoenobaenus*
A scarce passage migrant, most often seen between March and May, then again in September.

Marsh Warbler *Acrocephalus palustris*
This species owes its presence in the list to one record, from May 1971 (N-M), though it may well occur more regularly.

Reed Warbler *Acrocephalus scirpaceus*
A very numerous breeding species in the main reedbeds, with a season stretching from early March to early October. N-M estimates breeding density at around 19 pairs to the square kilometre.

Great Reed Warbler *Acrocephalus arundinaceus*
An other common breeding species, with a shorter season than the last species, and requiring a larger territory, as the size of the bird would suggest. At least two were singing at Santa Pola on 21st March, 1993, an early date for this species.

Olivaceous Warbler *Hippolais pallida*
Probably breeds in small numbers, in damp localities near the coast, but perhaps most likely to be seen during spring passage, especially on the coast and islands.

Melodious Warbler *Hippolais polyglotta*
A summer visitor to suitable locations, with an apparent preference for citrus plantations and scrub. Also a regular migrant, often to be seen in April.

Marmora's Warbler *Sylvia sarda*
One was seen and described at the Cabo de Santa Pola in October 1986, and there was a report of a skulking individual, probably of this species, near Relleu, in August 1989. Doubt has been cast on some recent sightings, and it is imperative that this species be seen — and heard — well, due to the considerable similarity of the next species in some plumages.

Dartford Warbler *Sylvia undata*
A common species indeed in the winter months. also breeds, though sparingly, at higher altitudes, and passes through as a passage migrant.

Spectacled Warbler *Sylvia conspicillata*
A difficult species to study, due to its retiring nature, but certainly present wherever *salicornia* flats are found, and almost certainly breeds commonly around El Hondo, the Torrevieja salt-lakes and at Santa Pola. also to be found on the island of Tabarca.

Subalpine Warbler *Sylvia cantillans*
A regular spring passage migrant, usually in April, and occasionally in full song. An adult at El Pinet on 7th March 1993, was very early. Breeds in the Sierras, but is never an easy bird to see.

Sardinian Warbler *Sylvia melanocephala*
Common and sedentary throughout the Province, occupying niches as diverse as montane scrub, gardens, field-edges, reedbeds and pinewoods.

Orphean Warbler *Sylvia hortensis*
A summer resident in small numbers, often in the valleys of the Sierras, where there are mature trees, and in olive-groves. May also be met with as a migrant on the coast.

Whitethroat *Sylvia communis*
A&G assert that this species is a rare breeder, and it may indeed have bred at Maigmó in 1989. As a bird of passage, of common occurrence, especially in spring.

Lesser Whitethroat *Sylvia curruca*
A very scarce migrant, averaging less than one record per annum, the latest to hand being one at San Vicente in October, 1991.

Garden Warbler *Sylvia borin*
A scarce passage migrant, tending to occur in May or October.

Blackcap *Sylvia atricapilla*
An abundant winter-visitor, seeming to take readily to a diet of dates, and therefore extremely numerous in the parks of Elche. Usually absent during the breeding season, but breeding apparently takes place just to the north, in Valencia.

Bonelli's Warbler *Phylloscopus bonelli*
A summer visitor and passage migrant in the Province. Most often, arrival is around late April or early May, but a male was in song at Maigmó on 26th March 1993. Return passage is usually during August/September.

Wood Warbler *Phylloscopus sibilatrix*
A frequent spring migrant, often present on Tabarca, especially in late April. Not nearly so common in autumn, but there are September records.

Chiffchaff *Phylloscopus collybita*
Present during the winter months — mainly between October and late February — in a wide variety of habitats, often reaching remarkable densities, especially in reedbeds, where plenty of insect food is available. Not normally encountered between mid-April and the end of September.

Willow Warbler *Phylloscopus trochilus*
Another common spring migrant, often to be heard in song during March and April in the lowland areas. Passage, however, appears to be quite rapid through the region. Returning birds may be found until quite late in October.

Goldcrest *Regulus regulus*
A scarce winter visitor, usually to the highlands, but also possible in coastal localities, from October to March.

Firecrest *Reulus ignicapillus*
A locally numerous resident of the Sierras, augmented by numbers from further north in the winter.

Spotted Flycatcher *Muscicapa striata*
A fairly numerous breeding species — restricted, no doubt, only by lack of mature woodland — and common passage bird, turning up as early as late March. Return passage is usually over by the end of September.

Pied Flycatcher *Ficedula hypoleuca*
A regular passage migrant, often in good numbers in autumn, especially at coastal localities. April and September are the best months, though migrants may still be found in October.

Bearded Tit *Panurus biarmicus*
A numerous resident of reedbeds at El Hondo, where a 1985 census recorded a minimum of 70 pairs. Whether numbers are higher or lower in winter, is difficult to establish, but the species is seldom abundant, and there may be some emigration outside the breeding season.

Long-tailed Tit *Aegithalos caudatus*
Not uncommon in the more wooded areas, both in coastal pinewoods and inland, where the species is more likely to be found in the summer months.

Crested Tit *Parus cristatus*
Quite a common resident of the high pinewoods, often seen in areas where thinner canopy allows some understorey. Occasionally wanders into the lowlands in winter.

Coal Tit *Parus ater*
Common in pine forests in the Sierras, especially in mature trees.

Blue Tit *Parus caeruleus*
Four at Denia in October 1989, and three near Villena in February 1991 are the only recent records to hand of this species, though nesting apparently occurs a little way to the north.

Great Tit *Parus major*
Common and well-distributed, occupying a wide variety of habitats.

Wallcreeper *Tichodroma muraria*
During the winters of 1991/2 and 1992/3, a single bird wintered on a rock-face near Sella. Were mountain areas to be better inspected at this season, it is possible that other wintering records may come to light.

Short-toed Treecreeper *Certhia brachydactyla*
Far from common, but may be met with almost anywhere, especially during its winter wanderings, when it may well be located in the pinewoods of the lower slopes of the mountains. Probably from necessity, the species appears to be restricted to pines in the Province.

Penduline Tit *Remiz pendulinus*
The 1985 census revealed some 35 pairs at El Hondo, and it is possible that numbers are augmented from further north outside the breeding season, when its call may be heard from reedbeds at Santa Pola and elsewhere.

Golden Oriole *Oriolus oriolus*
A scarce summer resident, most often to be found in the wooded valleys of the Sierras, but also on spring passage, often in coastal areas, in April or May.

Red-backed Shrike *Lanius collurio*
A very scarce and irregular migrant along the coastal strip, the most recent record being

of one at Santa Pola in October 1991.

Great Grey Shrike *Lanius excubitor*
A common resident in a variety of areas, frequenting agricultural areas as well as wilder country, probably increasing in winter, when it certainly spreads even more widely throughout the Province.

Lesser Grey Shrike *Lanius minor*
There is only one record of this attractive migrant, of one bird trapped at Crevillente on 2nd November 1990.

Woodchat Shrike *Lanius senator*
A very common summer visitor to many areas. An adult male at Santa Pola del Este on 8th March 1993 was remarkably early — more usually arrives in mid-April.

Jay *Garrulus glandarius*
Mentioned in A&G as a rare breeding species, and is certainly scarce, at best, as there appear to be few recent records of this relatively conspicuous species. One was near Petrer in May 1991, and one was heard at Miagmó in March 1993.

Magpie *Pica pica*
A local species in the Province, with a pocket of relative abundance in the valleys of the high Sierras to the south of Alcoy. Very uncommon in the southern lowlands.

Chough *Pyrrhocorax pyrrhocorax*
Almost certainly the most numerous corvid of the Province, with at least 3 colonies, the most observable being at Penaguila. Flocks outside the breeding season can reach 50 or more birds.

Jackdaw *Corvus monedula*
One or two widely distributed colonies are to be found in the area, but the species appears to be absent from a great many apparently suitable sites. Seems, in Alicante, to have a preference for the friable cliffs of clay found in some foothill locations, such as near to the Cuevas de Canalobre. Occasionally seen in good numbers around the Embalse de Pedrera, where a flock of 200 was present in January 1989.

Carrion Crow *Corvus corone*
A scarce and irregular visitor, probably not breeding in the Province. A record of 4 birds of the Hooded race *C.c.cornix,* near Petrer in March 1993, is awaiting acceptance. If granted this will be the first record of the subspecies for the Province.

Raven *Corvus corax*
A scarce breeding species, restricted, probably, to three or less pairs in the Sierras, with occasional sighting elsewhere.

Starling *Sturnus vulgaris*
An abundant winter visitor, with vast numbers roosting in the reedbeds of El Hondo, and smaller numbers to be met with almost anywhere. Arrival takes place from early October.

Spotless Starling *Sturnus unicolor*
A widely distributed breeding species, mainly in agricultural areas, with a tendency to wander in the winter months.

House Sparrow *Passer domesticus*
Common and numerous in towns and villages.

Tree Sparrow *Passer montanus*
A very scarce bird anywhere in the Province, with records restricted to that of a single bird in a flock of the last species, at Santa Pola in October 1987, until a pair was found to be breeding in isolated *Eucalyptus* trees, at El Hondo, in 1991. Four were nearby in early March, 1993.

Rock Sparrow *Petronia petronia*
A scarce breeding bird of the northern mountains, with small flocks to be found from the road to the northeast of Gorga. Common in parts of neighbouring Murcia Province. From time to time, may be looked for in more vegetated areas, and at lower altitudes, as evidence a flock near the Salinas de Torrevieja, in April 1990.

Common Waxbill *Estrilda astrild*
A small feral population of this African species appears to exist on low rocky hills in the neighbourhood of Pego.

Chaffinch *Fringilla coelebs*
In summer, a bird of the high pinewoods, but birds, probably largely from Northern Europe, are a common sight in lowland areas in winter, where birds start to arrive in early October.

Brambling *Fringilla montifringilla*
Two males were at La Marina, in a mixed flock of finches, in December 1991, on cultivated land.

Serin *Serinus serinus*
A very common resident in agricultural areas, particularly abundant in the citrus plantations of the south.

Greenfinch *Carduelis chloris*
A common resident in all parts of the Province, except, possibly, the highest mountains.

Goldfinch *Carduelis carduelis*
Numerous throughout the Province, though never abundant, probably due to persecution.

Siskin *Carduelis spinus*
An irregular migrant, most likely to be met with in March.

Linnet *Carduelis cannabina*
A well-dstributed species, occupying both agricultural areas and arid, rocky hillsides.

Crossbill *Loxia curvirostra*
Common in montane coniferous woodland, spreading erratically to coastal pines after the breeding season.

Trumpeter Finch *Bucanetes githagineus*
One was seen at Santa Pola in March 1988, then one (sexed as a male) on nearby Tabarca the following May. 1989 also saw two trapped near Monovar, both in spring, and a singing male, also in spring, in the Sierra de Crevillente. Although it is possible that some duplication may exist with the above records, it seems likely that the species may be in the process of establishing a foothold in the Province.

Hawfinch *Coccothraustes coccothraustes*
Eight adults of this species were captured and ringed at Monovar in September 1989, and one was seen at Elche in March of the same year.

Snow Bunting *Plectrophenax nivalis*
A male, trapped at the Embalse de la Pedrera, in February 1990, was the first inland record of this rather unexpected species, which has, however, occurred occasionally, on coasts further to the north.

Yellowhammer *Emberiza citrinella*
Two were at Petrel in early August, 1989, and one was at Denia in December, 1990, a more likely date for this northern species, perhaps.

Cirl Bunting *Emberiza cirlus*
An uncommon species across much of the region, with, however a good presence in the Jalon valley, where the wooded hillsides appear to be to this species' liking. Also found at the 'tree-line' on the Sierra de Aitana.

Rock Bunting *Emberiza cia*
Probably more common than it appears to be. This species may often be seen foraging around the base of pines in moderately dense woodland, and feeding with flocks of tits *Parus* in winter. Mainly found at higher altitudes, but lower down in winter.

Ortolan Bunting *Emberiza hortulana*
There is a scattering of — more-or-less annual — records of this species, usually on the coast, and in April.

Reed Bunting *Emberiza schoeniclus*
Reputed to have bred formerly, but certainly now a winter visitor to the wetlands, often in good numbers.

Corn Bunting *Miliaria calandra*
A common breeding bird in suitable agricultural habitat.

(285 species listed in the text)

CONSERVATION IN ALICANTE

Until quite recently, this would have been a very short chapter!

Even now, there have been relatively few initiatives which have had any effect in reducing disturbance, habitat-loss or hunting in the most sensitive parts of the Province.

The Spanish have gradually become aware of their unique natural history heritage with effect from, perhaps, the early seventies, since when political changes have had their effect, along with the growth of television, and, perhaps, the increasing awareness of the importance of their country to an ever-growing invasion of Northern European birders!

The first positive signs that things were looking up came in about 1990, when signs proclaiming 'Regional Park' status started to appear, both at Santa Pola and around the El Hondo marshes. Meanwhile, creeping development, agricultural encroachment and excessive hunting continue to take place all over!

We must, however, look on the bright side, and there is little doubt that there is a new realisation on the part of the authorities that measures need to be taken.

Elsewhere in the world, there is ample evidence that the establishment of 'visitor centres' and properly managed reserves can have a beneficial effect on a region's tourism. Alicante could certainly use a stimulation to low-season tourism, and it is incumbent upon those with an interest in wildlife to convince the authorities of the need for reserves to be established.

Pure altruism is unlikely to be the motive which achieves this, but if it could be shown that a 'market' exists . . .

The nearest thing to a reserve is that established at El Hondo in an uneasy partnership between private owners and the Valencian Environment Agency, but visiting is not really encouraged as yet, and a realisation of the commercial possibilities — if indeed they exist — has yet to dawn.

Here and elsewhere, the problems caused by clashes of interest between landowners, hunting syndicates and various governmental agencies are a long way from resolution.

Forgetting, for a moment, the harsh realities, it is clearly essential that development is checked in these sensitive coastal localities, and migrants, in particular, need frequent stopping-places along Mediterranean coastlines. Any pressure which can be brought to bear on appropriate bodies can only do good, and hopefully preserve this unique area for the enjoyment of future generations.

SPECIES CHECKLIST

Key to status summary:

- **R**   Resident throughout the year
- **RB**   Regular breeding visitor
- **OB**   Scarce or occasional breeding bird
- **W**   Winter visitor
- **M**   Passage migrant
- **V**   Vagrant or rare passage migrant
- **F**   Feral/introduced species
- **?**   Status uncertain

English name	Spanish name	Status
Red-throated Diver	Colimbo chico	V
Great Northern Diver	Colimbo Grande	V
Little Grebe	Zampullin chico	R, W. M
Great Crested Grebe	Somormujo grande	R, W, M
Black-necked Grebe	Zampullin cuellinegro	OB, W, M
Cory's Shearwater	Pardela cenicienta	M, ?
Mediterranean Shearwater	Pardela pichoneta	M, ?
Storm Petrel	Paino común	RB
Gannet	Alcatraz	W, M
Cormorant	Cormorán grande	W
Shag	Cormorán moñudo	?
Bittern	Avetoro	V
Little Bittern	Avetorillo	RB
Night Heron	Martinete	RB, M
Squacco Heron	Garcilla cangrejera	RB, M
Cattle Egret	Garcilla bueyera	R
Great White Egret	Garceta grande	V
Little Egret	Garceta común	R
Grey Heron	Garza reál	R, M, W
Purple Heron	Garza imperial	RB
Black Stork	Cigüeña negra	V
White Stork	Cigüeña blanca	V
Glossy Ibis	Morito	V
Spoonbill	Espátula	V
Greater Flamingo	Flamenco	OB, M, W
Lesser Flamingo	Flamenco enano	V
Greylag Goose	Ansar común	W
Ruddy Shelduck	Tarro canelo	V?
Shelduck	Tarro blanco	R, W
Wigeon	Anade silbón	W
Gadwall	Anade friso	OB, M, W
Teal	Cerceta común	W, M
Mallard	Anade reál	R, W
Pintail	Anade rabudo	W
Garganey	Cerceta carretona	OB, M
Shoveler	Pato cuchara	W
Marbled Duck	Cerceta pardilla	R
Red-crested Pochard	Pato colorado	R, W
Pochard	Porrón común	R, W
Ferruginous Duck	Porrón pardo	OB, V
Tufted Duck	Porrón moñudo	W

Common Scoter	Negrón común	V
Red-breasted Merganser	Serreta mediana	V
Ruddy Duck	Malvasia canela	V
White-headed Duck	Malvasia	OB
Honey Buzzard	Abejero	M
Black Kite	Milano negro	M
Red Kite	Milano reál	V
Griffon Vulture	Buitre leonado	V
Short-toed Eagle	Aguila culebrera	M, ?
Marsh Harrier	Aguilucho lagunero	OB, M, W
Hen Harrier	Aguilucho pálido	V
Montagu's Harrier	Aguilucho cenizo	M, ?
Goshawk	Azor	?
Sparrowhawk	Gavilán	?
Buzzard	Ratonero común	R, W
Spotted Eagle	Aguila moteada	W
Imperial Eagle	Aguila imperial	V
Golden Eagle	Aguila reál	?
Booted Eagle	Aguila calzada	M, ?
Bonelli's Eagle	Aguila perdicera	?
Osprey	Aguila pescadora	W
Lesser Kestrel	Cernicalo primilla	V
Kestrel	Cernicalo reál	R
Merlin	Esmerejón	W
Hobby	Alcotán	M
Eleonora's Falcon	Halcón de Eleonor	V
Peregrine	Halcón peregrino	?
Red-legged Partridge	Perdiz roja	R
Quail	Codorniz común	RB
Water Rail	Rascón	R
Spotted Crake	Polluela pintoja	M
Little Crake	Polluela bastarda	M, ?
Baillon's Crake	Polluela chica	OB, ?
Corncrake	Guión	V
Moorhen	Pollo de agua	R
Coot	Focha común	R
Crested Coot	Focha cornuda	?
Crane	Grulla común	V
Little Bustard	Sison	RB, ?
Oystercatcher	Ostrero	M, W
Black-winged Stilt	Cigüeñuela	RB, R
Avocet	Avoceta	R
Stone Curlew	Alcaraván	RB, ?
Collared Pratincole	Canastera	RB
Little Ringed Plover	Chorlitejo chico	M
Ringed Plover	Chorlitejo grande	M, W
Kentish Plover	Chorlitejo patinegro	R
Golden Plover	Chorlito dorado	W
Grey Plover	Chorlito gris	M, W
Lapwing	Avefria	W
Knot	Correlimos gordo	M
Sanderling	Correlimos tridáctilo	M, W

Little Stint	Correlimos meñudo	M, W
Temminck's Stint	Correlimos de Temminck	V?
Pectoral Sandpiper	Correlimos pectoral	V
Curlew Sandpiper	Correlimos zarapitin	M
Purple Sandpiper	Correlimos oscuro	V
Dunlin	Correlimos común	M, W
Ruff	Combatiente	M, W
Jack Snipe	Agachadiza chica	V
Snipe	Agachadiza común	W
Woodcock	Becada	W
Black-tailed Godwit	Aguja colinegra	W, M
Bar-tailed Godwit	Aguja colipinta	W, M
Whimbrel	Zarapito trinador	M
Curlew	Zarapito reál	M, W
Spotted Redshank	Archibebe oscuro	M, W
Redshank	Archibebe común	OB, M, W
Marsh Sandpiper	Archibebe fino	V
Greenshank	Archibebe claro	M, W
Green Sandpiper	Andarrios grande	M, W
Wood Sandpiper	Andarrios bastardo	M
Common Sandpiper	Andarrios chico	OB, M, W
Turnstone	Vuelvepiedras	M
Wilson's Phalarope	Falaropo de Wilson	V
Red-necked Phalarope	Falaropo picofino	M
Grey Phalarope	Falaropo picogrueso	V
Arctic Skua	Págalo párasito	W
Great Skua	Págalo grande	V
Mediterranean Gull	Gaviota cabecinegra	V
Laughing Gull	Gaviota reidora americana	V
Little Gull	Gaviota enana	M
Black-headed Gull	Gaviota reidora	R
Slender-billed Gull	Gaviota picofina	OB, W
Audouin's Gull	Gaviota de Audouin	R?, M
Common Gull	Gaviota cana	V
Lesser Black-backed Gull	Gaviota sombria	W
Herring Gull	Gaviota argentea	R
Iceland Gull	Gaviota polar	V
Great Black-backed Gull	Gavión	W
Kittiwake	Gaviota tridactila	V
Gull-billed Tern	Pagaza piconegra	M, ?
Caspian Tern	Pagaza piquirroja	M
Lesser Crested Tern	Charrán bengales	V
Sandwich Tern	Charrán patinegro	M, W
Common Tern	Charrán común	RB, M
Arctic Tern	Charrán artico	V
Little Tern	Charrancito	RB
Whiskered Tern	Fumarel cariblanco	RB
Black Tern	Fumarel común	OB, M
White-winged Black Tern	Fumarel aliblanco	V
Razorbill	Alca común	W
Black-bellied Sandgrouse	Ortega	RB
Rock Dove	Paloma bravia	R

English	Spanish	Status
Stock Dove	Paloma zurita	?
Woodpigeon	Paloma torcaz	OB?, M
Collared Dove	Tortola turca	?
Turtle Dove	Tortola común	RB, M
Monk Parakeet	Cotorrita gris	F?
Ring-necked Parakeet	Cotorra de Kramer	F?
Great Spotted Cuckoo	Crialo	OB?, M
Cuckoo	Cuco	RB
Barn Owl	Lechuza	R
Scop's Owl	Autillo	RB?
Eagle Owl	Buho reál	R?
Little Owl	Mochuelo común	R
Tawny Owl	Carabo común	R?
Long-eared Owl	Buho chico	OB?
Short-eared Owl	Buho campestre	W
Nightjar	Chotacabras gris	M
Red-necked Nightjar	Chotacabras pardo	RB
Swift	Venejo común	RB
Pallid Swift	Vencejo pálido	RB
Alpine Swift	Vencejo reál	RB?, M
Kingfisher	Martín pescador	R, W
Bee-eater	Abejaruco	RB, M
Roller	Carraca	OB?
Hoopoe	Abubilla	RB, R, M, W
Wryneck	Torcecuello	M, OB?
Green Woodpecker	Pito reál	R
Great Spotted Woodpecker	Pico picapinos	R
Calandra Lark	Calandria común	R
Short-toed Lark	Terrera común	RB
Lesser Short-toed Lark	Terrera marismeña	OB?
Crested Lark	Cogujada común	R
Thekla Lark	Cogujada montesina	R
Woodlark	Totovia	?
Skylark	Alondra común	W
Sand Martin	Avión zapador	RB, M
Crag Martin	Avión roquero	R, W
Swallow	Golondrina común	RB, M
Red-rumped Swallow	Golondrina daurica	RB, M
House Martin	Avión común	RB, M
Tawny Pipit	Bisbita campestre	M
Tree Pipit	Bisbita arboreo	M
Meadow Pipit	Bisbita común	W
Red-throated Pipit	Bisbita gorgirojo	V
Water Pipit	Bisbita ribereño	W
Yellow Wagtail	Lavandera boyera	RB, M
Grey Wagtail	Lavandera cascadena	M
White Wagtail	Lavandera blanca	R
Wren	Chorchín	R, W
Dunnock	Acentor común	V
Alpine Accentor	Acentor alpino	V
Rufous Bush Robin	Alzacola	RB
Robin	Petrirrojo	RB?, W

Nightingale	Ruiseñor común	RB, M
Bluethroat	Pechiazul	W
Black Redstart	Colirrojo tizón	R
Redstart	Colirrojo reál	M
Whinchat	Tarabilla nortena	M
Stonechat	Tarabilla común	R
Wheatear	Collalba gris	M
Black-eared Wheatear	Collalba rubia	RB
Black Wheatear	Collalba negra	R
Blue Rock Thrush	Roquero solitario	R
Rock Thrush	Roquero rojo	V
Blackbird	Mirlo común	R
Ring Ouzel	Mirlo capiblanco	M
Fieldfare	Zorzal reál	V
Song Thrush	Zorzal común	W
Redwing	Zorzal alirrojo	W
Mistle Thrush	Zorzal charlo	?
Cetti's Warbler	Ruiseñor bastardo	R
Fan-tailed Warbler	Buitrón	R
Grasshopper Warbler	Buscarla pintoja	M
Savi's Warbler	Buscarla unicolor	RB
Moustached Warbler	Carricerin reál	R?, M, W
Sedge Warbler	Carricerin común	M
Marsh Warbler	Carricero poliglota	M
Reed Warbler	Carricero común	RB, M
Great Reed Warbler	Carricero tordal	RB, M
Olivaceous Warbler	Zarcero pálido	RB, M
Melodious Warbler	Zarcero común	RB, M
Marmora's Warbler	Curruca sarda	V?
Dartford Warbler	Curruca rabilarga	R
Spectacled Warbler	Curruca tomillera	RB, ?
Subalpine Warbler	Curruca carrasqueña	M
Sardinian Warbler	Curruca cabecinegra	R
Orphean Warbler	Curruca mirlona	RB
Whitethroat	Curruca zarcera	M
Lesser Whitethroat	Curruca zarcerilla	V
Garden Warbler	Curruca mosquitera	M
Blackcap	Curruca capirotada	W
Bonelli's Warbler	Mosquitero papialbo	M, OB?
Wood Warbler	Mosquitero silbador	M
Chiffchaff	Mosquitero común	W
Willow Warbler	Mosquitero musical	M
Goldcrest	Reyezuelo sencillo	V?
Firecrest	Reyezuelo listado	R
Spotted Flycatcher	Papamoscas gris	RB, M
Pied Flycatcher	Papamoscas cerrojillo	M
Bearded Tit	Bigotudo	R
Long-tailed Tit	Mito	R
Crested Tit	Herrerillo capuchino	R
Coal Tit	Carbonero garapinos	R
Blue Tit	Herrerillo común	R?
Great Tit	Carbonero común	R

52

Wallcreeper	Treparriscos	V
Short-toed Treecreeper	Agateador común	R
Penduline Tit	Pájaro moscón	R, W
Golden Oriole	Oropendola	RB, M
Red-backed Shrike	Alcaudón dorsirrojo	V
Lesser Grey Shrike	Alcaudón chico	V
Great Grey Shrike	Alcaudón reál	R, W
Woodchat Shrike	Alcaudón común	RB
Jay	Arrendajo común	OB?
Magpie	Urraca	R
Chough	Chova piquirroja	R
Jackdaw	Grajilla	R
Carrion Crow	Corneja negra	OB?
Raven	Cuervo	R?
Starling	Estornino pinto	W
Spotless Starling	Estornino negro	R
House Sparrow	Gorrión domestico	R
Tree Sparrow	Gorrión molinero	V?
Rock Sparrow	Gorrión chillón	R
Common Waxbill	Astrilda común	F
Chaffinch	Pinzón común	R, M, W
Brambling	Pinzón reál	V
Serin	Verdecillo	R
Greenfinch	Verderón	R
Goldfinch	Jilguero	R
Siskin	Lúgano	M
Linnet	Pardillo común	R
Crossbill	Piquituerto común	R
Trumpeter Finch	Camachuelo trompetero	V?
Hawfinch	Picogordo	V?
Snow Bunting	Escribano nival	V
Yellowhammer	Escribano cerillo	V
Cirl Bunting	Escribano soteño	R
Rock Bunting	Escribano montesino	R
Ortolan Bunting	Escribano hortelano	M
Reed Bunting	Escribano palustre	W, ?
Corn Bunting	Triguero	R

Note: It is not suggested that this list is complete, due to limited watching in the past, but certainly represents the majority of species that may be seen. Additions from the category of 'vagrant' are always likely. Such species, and those marked as vagrants above, should be reported to:–

Anuario Ornitologico de la Comunidad Valenciana
C/Jacinto Benavente 8, 20.
Valencia 46005
Spain
(Tel: 96-374 9308)

REFERENCES AND ACKNOWLEDGEMENTS

No work of this kind can ever be complete, as bird populations change continually, and new observations come to light with regular effect.

Neither can such a summary be the work of one person, and the help of the following is gratefully acknowledged:–

R. Bailey, E. Baxter, B. Clarke, B. Conduit, G. Caldwell, C. Ellis, S. & K. Forselius, D. Hunter, D. Palmer, R. Palmer, A. Pay, K. Privett, A. Reese, A. J. Richards, T. Zaragozi and relatives.

One contribution, however, stands head and shoulders above the rest. The work of Jose Navarro Medina is scholarly enough in itself, but Jose's personal contribution, and some happy hours spent with him in the field, have convinced me of the need to try to reach a wider 'audience' than, sadly, can be reached by his own book, being, as it is, only available in Spanish.

Bibliography

Alvaraz & Gil-Delgado:	Aves nidificantes en la provincia de Alicante, Instituto Juan Gil-Albert, Alicante.
Calvo & Iborra:	Estudio ecologico de la Laguna de La Mata. Instituto Juan Gil-Albert, Alicante.
CODA-SEO:	Situacion de la avifauna de la Peninsula Iberica. CODA-SEO
Cramp et al:	Birds of the Western Palearctic. Oxford University Press.
J. D. Navarro Medina:	Estudio ornitologico de 'El Hondo.' Caja de Ahorros del Mediterraneo.

Anuarios Ornitologico Comunidad Valenciana (Annual Reports for the Valencian Community — published by the Estacion Ornitologica Albufera/Sociedad Espanola de Ornitologia, Av. Los Pinares 106, 46012 Valencia.

Grateful thanks are also due to Keith Privett, for correcting the proofs to the first edition, and for many helpful suggestions, and to Alan Richards, for similar services to the second edition.